P9-ECL-507

SANDSTONE SUNSETS

SANDSTONE SUNSETS

IN SEARCH OF EVERETT RUESS

BY MARK A. TAYLOR

GIBBS·SMITH
P
PUBLISHER

SALT LAKE CITY

First Edition

00 99 98 97 4 3 2 1

Text copyright © 1997 by Mark A. Taylor
Cover art copyright © 1997 by Randall Lake
Woodcut copyright © 1997 by Tom Olson

All rights reserved. No part of this publication may be
reproduced or transmitted in any form or by any means,
electronic or mechanical, without written permission
from the publisher, except brief excerpts for the purpose
of review.

This is a Peregrine Smith Book, published by
Gibbs Smith, Publisher
P.O. Box 667
Layton, UT 84041

Edited by Gail Yngve
Design by Kinde Nebeker
Cover art by Randall Lake, "Sunset at Davis Gulch"
Woodcut by Tom Olson

Printed and bound in the United States

Library of Congress Cataloging-in-Publication Data

Taylor, Mark A., 1949-
Sandstone sunsets : in search of Everett Ruess / by Mark Taylor.
—1st ed.
p. cm.
"This is a Peregrine Smith book"—T.p. verso
ISBN O-87905-803-X
1. Utah—Description and travel. 2. Ruess, Everett, b. 1914-
—Homes and haunts—Utah. 3. Taylor, Mark A., 1949-   —Journeys
—Utah. I. Title.
F826.T39   1997   97-741
917.9204'33—dc21   CIP

For my mother,
June Barnes Taylor
January 27, 1923–September 11, 1995

ACKNOWLEDGMENTS

Thanks to S. A. Taylor, Edith May Reynolds, Vikki Nelson, David Holbert, Ron Godfrey, Pennie Pace, Leslie Majors, Andrea Dumke, Fred Pace, Lana Mitchell, Bud Mixon, Robin Johnson, Mary Gaddie, Luke Valdez, Norma Higby, Iris Santos, Normalind Smith, Joy DeMaranville, Joel B. Zitting, Michael Hullet, Carol Bocchino, Nancy Brozovich, Chris Berger, Nancy Alvey, Sylvia Knight, Mick Tripp, Wendy Wood, Norma Mannos, Randall Potts, Travis Taylor, Zagg Taylor, Dina Bassett, and Gail Yngve for their help in the realization of this book.

Special thanks to Phil Sullivan, Randall Lake, Randy Godfrey, Grant Bassett, Roger Chapman, and Jeffrey Grathwohl. A very special thank you to Margo Taylor for believing in me and for sharing the vision of this work. This book would not have been possible without her.

PREFACE

In 1934, poet and adventurer Everett Ruess disappeared into southern Utah's red-rock country never to be seen again. Shortly before vanishing, Everett wrote of his affinity with nature and his love of the desert: "This trip will be longer than I expected, for I will be in many beautiful places, and do not wish to taste, but to drink deep."

Over the years, theories have been put forth, searches have been mounted, and books have been written, but the mystery of Everett Ruess remains unsolved. No matter how many times the facts have been circled up, they all lead back to the beginning. Could it be that Everett's is a mystery that should remain unsolved? The truth is, Everett left us years before he disappeared. His was a slow disappearing act, like the Anasazi footpaths fading into the blue dusk.

This year marks the tenth anniversary of my quest to find Everett. It is difficult to explain what gets under a person's skin and sets him or her off on the road to solve a puzzle or riddle that any reasonable person might quickly conclude was ill-advised or unsolvable. The inherent difficulty in making such explanations rests in the fact that usually the person making the inquiry doesn't know exactly why he or she is doing it.

When I began my quest, I had one set of objectives. These objectives revolved around the notion that I might be the person who could solve this fascinating puzzle. I believed I was qualified for this endeavor for two reasons: first, I was already an experienced investigative journalist; and second, I, too, had wandered this same landscape for many years. While the evidence and the circumstances pertaining to Everett's disappearance were either shrouded by time or lost altogether, I still believed that if I followed the surviving trail cairns back in time, I might be able to discover what happened to Everett at the end of his trail.

Strangely, somewhere along the pathway another set of objectives or imperatives appeared out on the horizon. These imperatives were highly personal, and, as a result, my search for Everett transformed into the search for something else as well. The following book is what I discovered, both about Everett and about my own undefined quest for personal understanding.

I will begin my story where Everett left us, on the outskirts of Escalante, Utah, in a grove of ancient cottonwood trees along the banks of the Escalante River. Under this soothing canopy, Everett watched the sun set on man's enterprise for the last time on November 11, 1934.

ESCALANTE, UTAH

An evening tempest caught in the canopy above, making the cottonwoods dip and roll, creating the sound of a river rushing down a steep canyon. In the tempest's wake, I listened to the mix of sounds Everett might have heard there—the lazy Escalante River rolling over worn sandstone steps, the expert rapping of a carpenter's hammer on wood, a steer bellowing from some far-off pasture. Another gust swept through the grove, this time lifting and swirling the treetops and forcing the great trunks to bend all the way to the ground. With the wind at my back, I turned away from the Escalante to search the horizon of this wilderness.

This land did not give up its secrets willingly; it exacted a price from those who sought to discover the source of its allure and power. Today, this land signified more the contemporary view of transcendence than perhaps any other place on earth. Everett was not the first to be drawn here nor will he be the last. Men have searched this outback for pieces of their soul. They arrived restless and left changed.

After nightfall I made a campfire near the river and slept next to it. In the morning, I bade farewell to the cottonwood grove and the town of Escalante with its worn-out pastures, its rust-encrusted farm equipment—frozen in place like Oz's Tin Man—and to its oozing barrels of petroleum waste, leaching into the ground behind a long-closed gas station on Main Street.

I plunged into the desert wilderness, driving down the Hole in the Rock trail, following Everett's path to the last place he was known to be seen. The dirt road welcomed me. There were few signs of man out there, only the dusty dirt road that circled the landscape like a cowboy's lasso. In the sky above, an occasional airliner glinted in the sun, perfect silver crucifixes pointing west. I slowly turned the radio dial. Nothing but static. Good. At the end of the dial, I picked up a faint signal from St. George, Utah, some one hundred miles to the west. The radio announcer almost seemed to brag, "Today's high will top 110 degrees, even hotter out in the deserts."

Whatever happened out here on this landscape millions of years ago was cataclysmic. Cauldrons of red-hot pig iron poured over the land; oceans flooded, flourished, and receded; great land masses buckled up and became cannon fodder for volcanic artillery pieces, and now it all lies in repose, strewn haphazardly across the landscape. An easy peace mantles the corpses of this Armageddon today. The rain and wind have softened its edges, and time has brought the beauty of decay.

Everett visited red-rock country for the first time in 1931 and immediately knew he belonged there. Until he disappeared, he ranged over the sagebrush and cedar forests, climbed the towering ridges, and explored the deep winding canyons. While fascism blossomed in Europe and the grapes of wrath ripened in the American dust bowl, young Everett Ruess beat a solitary path into the heart of this expansive wilderness.

In late autumn 1934, with only his burros as companions, Everett traveled down the old Mormon Hole in the Rock trail on his way to the Grand Canyon. His plan was to winter in the hidden canyons of the Escalante Drainage and Glen Canyon. Few men had visited these narrow winding canyons since the ancient Anasazi Indians lived in them hundreds of years earlier.

By mid-afternoon, I arrived at a deserted camp where ten days after he departed Escalante, Everett camped with two sheepherders. Five months later, in the wet spring of 1935, the sheepherders told searchers that he left their camp on the morning of November 17, heading east in the direction of Davis Gulch. It is the last time he is known to have been seen.

No one knows how long Everett stayed in Davis Gulch before he vanished—leaving behind little more than his footprints in the deep sand to be found the next spring. Even though Everett's vanishing act began earlier, it was accomplished here. Remarkably, the last real word from him still makes the journey back to us today. Through his letters, poems, and essays—composed for family and friends—he beckons us forward today; he invites us to join him on the pathway across the land he loved so intensely.

The view from the sheepherder's camp was spectacular. To the west, less than a half mile away, the cliffs of Fifty Mile Ridge dominated the horizon and appeared more like some exaggerated Hollywood backdrop than a world-class buttress of Kayenta sandstone. To the north, east, and southeast, the land was an endless jumble of deep winding gorges and canyons that cut through a seventy-five-square-mile tract of broken rock and petrified sand dunes. To the south, twenty miles away, Navajo Mountain climbed nearly 10,000 feet and set an anchor in the sky. The Navajo gods lived there.

Six months before his disappearance, Everett camped on Navajo Mountain.

In a letter to a friend, he wrote about the place where he eventually disappeared: "The country to the north is as rough and impenetrable a territory as I have ever seen. Thousands of domes and towers of sandstone lift their rounded pink tops from blue and purple shadows."

I explored the campsite in the blistering heat, sensing his presence. "I know what happened to you," I said out loud. I am convinced the original search conducted in March of 1935 and the subsequent searches that summer were not only flawed but totally inadequate. For the last ten years I have conducted my own painstakingly slow but thorough search of the area. I have made discoveries and tracked down leads where no one expected to find them. I have even developed my own theory about Everett's disappearance, and now—like all good investigators—I have set out to disprove myself.

After dark, I did not build a campfire. Instead, I spread a tarpaulin and lay on my back, hands clasped behind my head. The silence and the starry sky calmed me. At sunrise, I carefully packed my daypack and started off for Davis Gulch. The first few hours were delightful, and I was filled with a youthful confidence, but by 10:30 A.M., the temperature neared 100 degrees and waves of heat shimmered off the superheated surfaces of the sandstone.

Few explorers are foolhardy enough to venture into the desert at this time of the year—and to hike alone, where a simple turned ankle could spell disaster, was taking an enormous risk. In my twenty years of wandering this red-rock canyon country, I have taken many calculated risks; this would be another. I was as prepared as anyone could be for all contingencies, or so I thought.

Davis Gulch was formed by water from rain or melting snow rushing off the mesa tops and cutting a deep, narrow gorge through the soft sandstone on its way to the Colorado River and now the man-made Lake Powell miles downstream. To get to Everett's last campsite, I would work my way down from the plateau top through the dangerous narrows of the gulch and then into the main canyon below. The narrows could present serious problems, yet once negotiated the gulch widened and became enchanting. The Anasazi Indians lived in the canyon bottom, as did old West outlaws wanting to make themselves scarce.

Before descending into the intestine-like narrows, I took a fix on my location. My reference point would be Fifty Mile Ridge to the west. Once I was in the deep canyon, it would be of no use to me, but somewhere below I would climb back out, locate my reference point, and make my way to it. I proceeded with great caution. Some say the narrows are impassable, while others maintain that a strong agile person can make it. At first, the narrows were quite straight and I could see hundreds of feet ahead and behind me, but then slowly they narrowed, finally corkscrewing and making cowlick-like turns where I could see only a few feet ahead or behind.

It was cool in the narrows, perhaps thirty degrees cooler than on the plateau. In my sight, the sky was reduced to a blue ribbon running between the canyon walls hundreds of feet above. The passageway slowly closed in on me and, at times, I was forced to take my pack off, turn sideways, and squeeze through. My breathing was labored, and it felt as if some heavy weight pressed against my chest. Did Everett come this way, I wondered? What did he feel here?

Somewhere below, the narrows would widen and a year-round creek with lush greenery growing along its length would make this dangerous part of the hike worthwhile. From there, the narrows would be viewed as an adventure. This line of reasoning offered some comfort until, rounding a corner, I discovered an enormous choke stone wedged across my path. The triangular-shaped boulder had fallen from the cliff tops above and was wedged in such a way that there was no way to climb over it. There was, however, just enough room to squirm under it. A part of me wanted to retreat, but I would not give in to my fears. Lying on my back in the sand, I shimmied under the ten-ton boulder's darkened mass. Sweat pooled in my eye sockets. Fear tightened my chest. What if the boulder slips and crushes me, I asked myself. I could feel the weight of the stone on my chest. I couldn't breathe but still moved forward quickly.

Safely on the other side, I found no relief from my fear. Instead, I discovered another obstacle: a twenty-foot drop-off with a plunge pool at the bottom, filled with stagnant and primordial water; it smelled ghastly. I languished there far too long before wedging myself between the canyon walls, a technique called friction climbing, and began working my way down. Halfway to the bottom, a horrible thought occurred to me: what if the pool of water was so deep it was over my head? Furthermore, if the narrows were really impassable, then the drop-off I was descending would become a jump-up—a much more difficult obstacle to negotiate when coming back. With my back against one canyon wall and my hands and knees straining against the other, I paused to consider my predicament. I had cast my lot; there was nothing for me to do but continue. At the bottom, I was happy to discover the pool was only knee deep.

For the next hour or so, I proceeded slowly, working my way over and under choke stones, wedging my way down drop-offs, and moving cautiously forward. The narrows widened a bit, arced to the left, then opened into a long straightaway. I moved forward to its end when suddenly I heard a voice! That is, I believed I heard a voice. I froze and strained to listen—

nothing except my breathing and the pounding of my heart. I moved slowly forward, then heard it again. It was a voice, a human voice! It was growing clearer and coming up the narrows towards me.

"I'll bet no one has ever been this way before," a man's voice said.

I was stunned and responded without thinking. "Except for me, of course."

Silence.

"Anyone there?" I finally asked.

"Is someone up ahead of us?" a woman asked.

"Just li'l ol' me," I said. I was trying to sound friendly, but I felt annoyed. My adventure was devalued. I had traveled to one of the most remote and inaccessible places in North America; I had faced dangerous predicaments for the purpose of being alone. Damn!

I heard other voices. They were low and heavy, like people discussing something of gravity. Finally, a man's voice rose up, "I just don't believe it!"

I leaned against the sandstone and waited. A man appeared in the narrow passageway ahead of me. He reminded me of Vincent van Gogh, had van Gogh lived to be seventy-five. Behind him was a woman about the same age. We exchanged introductions. They were the Shaws, Don and Thelma, from California. Around the corner, hidden from view, were Helen, their daughter-in-law, and Kathrine, a family friend. They were vacationing with friends on Lake Powell some miles away.

It was difficult for me to fathom how this unlikely group of novices came to Davis Gulch. Even more perplexing was how they were able to climb up the narrows. I learned later it was their complete naivete combined with Don's insistence that they continue that had brought them to me. When Helen and Kathrine finally came into view, I could see the signs of fear and exhaustion on their faces. They were good looking, tanned, and pampered, yet they were troubled and covered with scrapes and abrasions from head to toe.

For their part, they were incredulous that I was in the narrows alone, searching for some unknown poet who had been missing for nearly six decades. They advised me not to proceed. Glancing over her shoulder, Thelma told me, "Mark, you'll never make it alone."

Don and I had a short discussion about what was on the plateau above. I suggested they turn around and that we all go back down through the narrows and into the gulch. "It will be even more difficult getting back to the lake over the petrified sand dune above," I said.

"I'll never go back there again! Never!" Helen said.

I was faced with my first real dilemma. If they were not going to follow me, I felt obligated to follow them, at least until I understood more about their plans. These people were not my responsibility. Still, with the intense heat and their unfamiliarity with the area, I believed they could be in serious trouble. I would be negligent, even criminal, not to assist them.

Two hours later, out of the narrows, we rested on a petrified sand dune resembling an enormous cow pie. Every year, Don and Thelma vacationed on Lake Powell, each time visiting another canyon or secluded alcove. Arguably, the lake is one of the most beautiful in the world, and it has grown into a recreationalists' mecca. But it is highly unlikely that in today's environmental arena, the Glen Canyon Dam would have ever gotten off the drawing board.

Straddling the Utah-Arizona border, the Glen Canyon Dam has two primary purposes: to supply southern California and many other western communities with cheap hydroelectric power and to serve as an upper-basin holding reservoir for storing water during the wet seasons to be released to the lower basins in drier seasons. Many in the West, especially Californians, enjoy an economic energy resource, and hundreds of thousands of them vacation on the lake every year.

With visitation comes litter, overcrowding, and the development of industrial tourism. In a way, California recreationalists also bring their air pollution with them, carried on the prevailing west-to-east winds. Southern California pollution seriously degrades air quality and reduces visibility over the entire Four Corners area, including six national parks.

Construction of the Glen Canyon Dam was met with little resistance from the puny and still wet-behind-the-ears 1950s environmental forces. The subordination of this land and the destruction of its archaeological treasures by filling the spectacular canyon is still hotly debated today. Geologically speaking, Glen Canyon's significance rivaled that of Canyonlands National Park to the north and Grand Canyon National Park to the south.

My thoughts returned to my new companions, sitting around me on the sand dune. They looked tired and thirsty. I offered them water, and they gulped it down greedily; they had been six hours without a drink. Then I offered them apples, cheese, crackers, and more water from my daypack. They were sunburned so I gave them sunscreen as well as Band-Aids and salve for their injuries. I offered Don my extra shirt, giving Kathrine the one I wore; she was in a bikini top and shorts. Her shoulders were already glowing with sunburn. My extra socks and sunglasses went to Thelma, but there was nothing I could do for Helen. Helen was wearing a pair of blue plastic slip-on shoes and no socks. Her feet were red and swollen.

"They only cost me two dollars," she said.

I could not withhold my bewilderment any longer, "I can't believe you guys. You are totally unprepared. Look at me, I have hiking boots, water— fact is, you need a minimum of one gallon of water per person per day—I have food, rope, tools, and topographical maps. Whether you know it or not, hiking this country is very dangerous. If you aren't properly prepared, you're risking your lives."

No one has the right to be unprepared, I said to myself. Yet, I was there alone—a sin of the highest order.

My outburst surprised them, but they didn't act resentful. They seemed unaware of the danger and did not fully appreciate my concern. Thelma explained that when they left the boat at 6:30 A.M., it was cool and they had planned to hike only a few hours. "That's why we didn't bring anything with us," she said.

I sensed that Don did not take what I said seriously. After all, why should he? I was out there alone, and if it was as dangerous as I made out, what was I doing there? Perhaps I was the one whose judgment should be questioned.

Thelma, Helen, and Kathrine were bone-tired, but surprisingly Don (I was to learn later, a self-made millionaire) appeared fresh and undaunted. Don's plan was to hike to the top of the gulch and then return via a trail he believed was on the plateau above. Don had been in the area once years earlier and was convinced a trail, located to the northwest, would lead them back to the lake.

Don was incorrect, and I told him so. We consulted my topographical map. It showed no trail. Still, Don insisted it was there. I knew that if they hiked northwest it would take them farther away from the lake and into a maze of sandstone formations known for swallowing up livestock. The sun-bleached bones of many desert-wise cattle litter the area—Everett's bones may well be among them.

Again, I attempted to convince these intelligent people to go back through the narrows. "It is the fastest and safest way," I said, but they would have nothing to do with it. One trip through the narrows was quite enough, thank you.

If Don had his way, there was an excellent chance they would join Everett somewhere out there. To complicate matters, none of them had yet grasped the tragic implications of their folly so they didn't ask me for help. I had no choice; I had to stay with them whether they wanted me to or not.

"If you're not going back the way you came, let me lead you back along the canyon rim." I pulled out my map and with my finger followed the canyon ridge toward Lake Powell. To my surprise, the women eagerly accepted my offer. Don looked down at the sandstone and said nothing. I knew there was no path leading back to the lake as Don believed, and if they were not going to return the way they came, then following the canyon rim was the next best plan.

If they returned via the narrows, it would mean another six-mile hike, but following the canyon rim and being forced to detour around intersecting canyons makes the return distance several miles longer. To make matters worse, they had already hiked many miles in the treacherous heat, and we had very little water left. I tried to sell the narrows one more time, but it was no use. I had cast my lot and perhaps my life with this group of neophytes.

The path I picked was not easy, and our progress was slow and hard won. Time and again, we were forced to detour around deep, narrow tributary canyons intersecting Davis Gulch. Periodically, we stopped to rest in the shade of rock outcroppings. We finished off the last of the water. It was hot but, oh, so delicious. As the others rested I scouted ahead, exploring the tributaries, hoping to find a quick and safe way down into the gulch.

Back on the trail, as a diversion I told them how in March of 1935, after Everett had been missing for four months, a search party comprised of farmers from Escalante found his two burros in Davis Gulch. The animals were alive, well, and in a man-made corral. This offered hope that Everett would be found alive as well. Searchers followed his footprints along the canyon bottom. They located his campsites, found his tin cans, and even found a place where they believed he had left a cryptic message scrawled into a soft sandstone wall. The message read: "NEMO was here. Nov. 1934." But Everett Ruess was not to be found.

The mystery became even more perplexing when searchers could not find his camp equipment and personal belongings. The authorities were stumped. Some speculated Everett was killed by a rustler or renegade Navajo who buried the body and took his belongings. Others theorized that he fell from one of the thousands of cliffs in the area and was never found. This theory has merit; in a letter to his brother, Waldo, in 1934, Everett wrote: "Many times in the search for water holes and cliff dwellings, I trusted my life to crumbling sandstone and angles little short of the perpendicular, startling myself when I come out whole and on top."

Those who believe Everett perished from a fall explain his missing belongings by maintaining that they are still out there somewhere. If these believers are right, Everett's 1934 journal would be there, too. If his journal were found, it might offer clues to what happened to him. It would undoubtedly fetch a hefty price in the publishing business.

Still, there are others who believe that when the first two searchers from Escalante entered Davis Gulch, they quickly located Everett's camp and equipment. They could see that he had not been there for a long time and concluded he was not coming back. At that point, they divided his goods and kept quiet.

The Shaws and I marched on mile after circuitous mile, detour after detour. The water was long gone. My mouth was so dry I tried an old Boy Scout trick, sucking on a small pebble. I wouldn't advise doing this though; the soft sandstone disintegrates in the mouth. By late afternoon, the first signs of dehydration appeared. Our pace slowed to a crawl. Once, after a short rest, Don hiked off back the way we had just come. Another time, he pointed to a rock outcropping on the horizon and suggested we hike over to it to get a better look.

"But, Don," I said, "between where we are standing and where you are pointing there is a canyon, hundreds of feet deep." I invited him to look at the map, which he did, but he still insisted we could "just walk right over there." I suggested he go take a look. When he returned he seemed genuinely perplexed and admitted there was indeed a canyon.

We entered into an area where freestanding spires and fins reached to the sky. It was difficult not to see the resemblance these formations had to sexual body parts. Enormous phalluses jostled in position at the edge of huge breast-shaped domes with cleavages beckoning. Twisted rocks with fashionable posteriors, some with gaping vaginas or mooning rectums, invited further exploration. Even the fin-shaped formations were reminiscent of our once-aquatic erogenous apparatus; before this land was formed, we swam great oceans and our dorsals were a main attraction.

In July 1935, after three quasi-official searches failed to solve the mystery of Everett's disappearance, ace reporter John Upton Terrell was dispatched from the *Salt Lake Tribune* to investigate. Because neither Everett nor his equipment had been found, many believed he was still alive. Some romantics theorized Everett married a beautiful Navajo maiden and was living in secrecy on the Navajo Reservation. Terrell enlisted help from three Navajos, one a famous tracker named Dougi, and the others a very powerful medicine man, Natani, and his psychic wife. After chanting and praying, Natani told Terrell, "He [Everett] has gone away and does not mean to come back." Asked if that meant Everett was dead, the shaman responded, "There is a shadow and I do not see clearly. I only say that he has gone away, and he went from where he camped."

Dougi, who was already famous for tracking down outlaws and desperados a generation earlier, traveled with Terrell to Davis Gulch and conducted his own search. After several days in the canyon and on the plateau above, Dougi was stumped. He had found many signs of Everett that had been overlooked by the previous search parties. He found Everett's footprints miles away at the Hole in the Rock overlook and again at the base of Fifty Mile Ridge at the top of Davis Gulch. Dougi even found the exact place where, eight months earlier, Everett had laid his bedroll for the last time. Still, no clear picture emerged. He told Terrell,

> "Everett did not go south or east into Navajo land, and there is no sign of him going north or west."

> "Could he have been killed and buried in Davis Gulch?" Terrell asked.

> "No," Dougi said, "I would have easily found his grave."

As Don, Thelma, Helen, and Kathrine shuffled along, I anxiously scouted ahead. If I could just find a way into the canyon, our worries would be over. A vertical drop of only 300 feet separated us from water and safety. We were so close yet so far. When I returned from one such scouting venture, I found Don, Thelma, and Helen moving off to the northwest in the direction of Don's nonexistent trail. I assured them it couldn't be much farther, and if they followed me, I could guarantee success. Thelma and Helen looked at me with relief in their faces, yet Don only reluctantly rejoined the group.

It was difficult for Don to relinquish control to me—or I suspect to anyone—perhaps as difficult as it would be for me to relinquish control to him. I was a reluctant participant in our little battle of the wills, but by then, I too had a vested interest in the outcome.

After a particularly long and difficult stretch with the sun beating down unmercifully, the group rested and I explored yet another dangerous-looking chasm nearby. I moved quickly down a series of steep, dry, stair-like waterfalls, each with a plunge pool at the bottom—a total of perhaps 200 vertical feet. At the last plunge pool, I found a 100-foot drop-off. There would be no getting into the gulch this way.

I turned and began to climb back out when, to my utter horror, I found I couldn't get out. In my haste, I had scurried down the steep rock face without thinking about climbing back out. Again and again, I threw myself against the nearly vertical walls, but each time I fell back—once, nearly plummeting off the cliff. Was this what happened to Everett, I wondered? My folly was compounded because I had left my daypack with rope inside with the others. I had prepared for this day for years, but now that it was here, I found myself unprepared. My pack and its contents would be of no use to me. I yelled to the others and waited, but no one came. They had deserted me.

A half hour later, as I frantically notched footholds in the sandstone with the can opener on my Swiss Army knife, I heard Kathrine calling for me.

"Down here!" I cried out.

Kathrine retrieved my daypack and threw down the rope so I could hoist my dumb ass out. By the time we made it back to where the others should have been, they were gone. I scrambled to the top of a giant cow-pie formation and scanned the horizon. I called out but only silence answered.

There was no time to waste. Without water there was little chance that Don, Thelma, and Helen would make it. Kathrine and I hiked as quickly as the terrain allowed. Earlier, I had marshaled my energy, but now it was time to go for broke. For more than two hours we kept up a grueling pace, covering a tremendous amount of country. Fatigue plagued us. We were desperate for water. The heat was excruciating. My arms hung like giant holiday hams from my torso, and my legs burned to the marrow.

Finally, at the place where even good-natured people turned nasty, just before the juncture where exhaustion and defeat collide, an obvious path appeared below us leading down into Davis Gulch. We had won. I cried out. "Gawd damned, we made it!" Kathrine and I embraced.

Once in the cool canyon bottom, our hopes were buoyed and we made tracks down the gulch to the lakeshore. I was dizzy, light-headed, and sick to my stomach. When we finally reached the lake we stripped down and dove into the cool blue water. I had long resented this lake, but now it was sublime beyond measure. Within a few seconds, I cramped up and had to work hard just to climb out.

It had been twelve hours since Don, Thelma, Helen, and Kathrine left for a morning hike, and the members of their party were frantic. When we arrived at their boat, Doug, Don and Thelma's son and Helen's husband, was preparing to hike up the gulch. If we had been ten minutes later, he would have hiked four or five miles up Davis Gulch only to reach the narrows after sunset.

It was 6:30 P.M., too late for the authorities to mount a search before nightfall but not too late to climb back onto the plateau and make one last attempt to find them. I gave Doug my map and pinpointed the place they might be if they continued in a northwesterly direction from where we separated.

Doug was drunk. He had marked the waiting time drinking highballs. Worse, his eyes swam across the features of the map, and he admitted to me, "I have never hiked in the desert before."

This was not good, but I said nothing. Doug's family was in grave danger and they needed his help. I watched him start up the steep rock face leading to the plateau, carrying a gallon of water and a marine radio; as he went I wondered if he, too, would become a victim. It was obvious that Kathrine and I suffered from exhaustion and dehydration, yet I promised to follow him onto the plateau after a little rest and rehydration.

A half hour later, I started my slow ascent up the switchback incline. I was slaphappy from exhaustion and dizzy from the heat. I felt hollow and feared I would pass out. One foot in front of the other, I kept telling myself. I, too, carried a gallon of water and a marine radio, and just as I reached the plateau above, Doug's excited voice came over his radio. He had found his father wandering across the superheated, petrified sand dunes. At first, Don neither recognized his son nor did he know who or where Thelma and Helen were.

When I arrived, Don was sitting on a large flat stone by himself. Doug had gone on ahead, attempting to locate the others.

"There was no trail," Don said as I approached.

I was angry and wanted to say, I told you so. Don was very weak but assured me he would be all right, so I left him there and moved off into the desert.

It was dusk and the landscape was submerged in a hot, golden marmalade atmosphere. Large sandstone formations miles away appeared closer than smaller ones just hundreds of yards away. The dusk was so beautiful, I was transfixed, gazing out into the wild and unreal light. I had a strong desire to sit down and consider eternity. But tonight, eternity would have to wait; there was less than one hour to find Thelma and Helen and return to the lake. I pushed onward, every footfall feeling like ten.

It was a mistake for me to be there. My eyes were playing tricks on me. I saw Everett standing at the bottom of a ledge, smiling up at me; but when I looked again, he was gone. I knew my search for Everett had become more important than finding him. It was clear that Everett should remain missing and I should continue searching. The pursuit of his silhouette standing at the next horizon was fulfillment enough. I was on the right pathway.

Still, I pushed onward, my equilibrium impaired and my ability to make judgements gone. Doug's voice came over the radio again; he had located Thelma and Helen, but something was wrong. He was frantic; his mother was unconscious. She had lain down in the shade of a rock outcropping and now could not be roused.

Luckily, by the time I arrived Thelma was conscious again and sitting up. She suffered from exposure and disorientation. "You saved us, Mark!" she cried out when I appeared on a hilltop. Thelma could not walk unassisted, so I put my arm around her and she put her arm around me and we walked back together. Helen's feet were so badly injured by her plastic, two-dollar shoes that Doug piggybacked her the entire way back.

CHAPTER TWO

BACK IN ESCALANTE

That night I rested on an air mattress in the bow of Don and Thelma's quarter-million-dollar boat. I was exhausted but sleep would not come. I watched stars sweep across the sky, from horizon to horizon, in a race to infinity—a race where winners place dead last.

Someone approached from the boat's stern. It was Don. Since returning to the safety of the boat, Don had been quiet—so quiet—in fact, everyone was worried; but no one—not even Thelma—ventured near him.

"Mark, are you awake?" Don asked.

"Yes."

"I was wrong, Mark," he said in the halting manner of men of my father's generation who gag on such words as "sorry," "wrong," "love."

I quickly got to my feet, and we embraced. When I pulled back, I was startled by what I saw. In the starlight Don had transformed into Achilles from Homer's *Iliad*. Tanned, bearded, and wearing a loose-fitting white muslin robe, Achilles stood before me. Don was ageless, like the stars.

The next morning long before the sun reached into the canyon bottom, I was on my way. I did not go back the way I came, choosing instead to skirt around the petrified sand dunes and make my way back to the road. From the plateau above, I measured the distance to my reference point, Fifty Mile Ridge. It was many miles away. As I stood there surveying the prospect of this land, I noticed a faint trail to the northwest. Time and the elements had nearly obliterated it. Don had been right—there was indeed a trail. Unfortunately, this trail would not have helped my new friends. Later, I learned it was an Anasazi trail, perhaps the same one Everett followed on his way into eternity.

I didn't make it back to my car until late afternoon. The long hot hike left me weak and dazed. I pulled a cold beer from my cooler and collapsed on a mound of soft bronze sand where I gazed out over the land. A few minutes later, the shadow of Fifty Mile Ridge tapped me on the shoulder. It had been stalking me, stealing through the bushes and moving along the game trails. I didn't fight the shadow, moving into the sunlight as is my usual manner. Instead, I submitted to it and, in doing so, became part of it. Together, we raced eastward, changing every facet of the land as we went. We turned the tops of sagebrush aqua blue, we created seams in the smooth sandstone, and we closed all the canyon entrances for the night.

The dominion of dusk was firmly in control, yet on a far-off plateau maybe seventy-five miles away, a castle of Navajo sandstone blazed like fire with the last rays of sunlight. The castle stood against the dusk, as if to say, "This moment is mine! Watch me burn." In the time it took to drink a beer, the castle transformed into the blades of many knives. The blades cut and tore into the new night, spilling out the purple haze.

"Good night, Everett," I called out.

Back in Escalante, nerves were on edge. Word was out that radical environmentalists from EarthFirst! had burned two remote line shacks and shot twenty-five head of cattle grazing on Bureau of Land Management (BLM) land.

Some cowboys congregated in the middle of Main Street, eyeballing everyone who drove by. At the curb, their four-wheelers stood at attention, lever-action Winchester 94s racked up in rear windows. Not knowing the score, I cruised by slowly, nodding my head and trying to see what all the commotion was about. An air of disgust expanded the cowboys' checkered shirts—I was not one of them. I was suspect. A few pushed large bony fists deep into shallow, faded Levi's pockets; others tilted their heads cockeyed.

The town of Escalante is struggling to remain the friendly little farm and ranch community Everett found in 1934. Back then, when Everett arrived astride one of his two burros, he was welcomed into the bosom of the tightly knit community. In his last-known letter written to his brother, Waldo, and posted on November 11, 1934, Everett spoke about the people of Tropic and Escalante, two Mormon communities:

> I stopped a few days in a little Mormon town and indulged myself in family life, church-going, and dances. If I had stayed any longer I would have fallen in love with a Mormon girl, but I think it's a good thing I didn't. I've become a little too different from most of the rest of the world.

Today, these hard-working people are caught between their beloved lifestyle of farming, ranching, mining, and logging, and the reality of the new-world environmental movement. Not long ago, the canyons and plateaus seemed to stretch far beyond the multi-horizons. Those who accepted the challenges pushed back the emptiness and carved out a place for themselves.

The canyon-country land dispute, which has smoldered since the construction of Glen Canyon Dam, has now ignited and could well blow up into an old-fashioned western land war. Sadly, there is little common ground between traditional land users and their environmental counterparts. If Everett wandered into Escalante today, he would most likely be considered an outsider. Ironically, Everett's love of the land would be widely accepted by both groups. Again, from his last-known letter, written nearly six decades ago:

> As to when I shall visit civilization, it will not be soon, I think. I have not tired of the wilderness; rather I enjoy its beauty and the vagrant life I lead, more keenly all the time. I prefer the saddle to the streetcar, the star-sprinkled sky to a roof, the obscure and difficult trail, leading into the unknown, to any paved highway, and the deep peace of the wild to the discontent bred by cities.

After passing the locals on Main Street, I drove to the old Bailey house at the edge of town and parked. Gail Bailey was the first man into Davis Gulch, and he found Everett's burros. The house was old and leaned heavily into itself as if it might collapse. Instead of getting out of my car, I sat back and let my eyes trace over every inch of its outline, especially the attic.

Over the years, allegations have continued to surface, claiming that when Everett's burros were discovered in Davis Gulch, his belongings were found as well. These allegations first came from members of the original search party itself. Privately, several searchers accused two or perhaps three fellow searchers of finding Everett's gear and splitting it up between them. By today's standard, Everett had little of value: two beautiful Navajo blankets, painting equipment, a box camera, a small amount of cash, the burros, cooking equipment, and, of course, his journal.

While not a single piece of evidence supporting these allegations has surfaced, some locals insist they are true. If someone did divide up Everett's goods, perhaps some of his belongings survived and are hidden in one of the original searcher's house. All but two of the original searchers populate the Escalante Cemetery, and the survivors have long refused further comment about the alleged incident. It is known that when Gail Bailey entered Davis Gulch, he quickly took charge of Everett's burros and kept them. This could be viewed as an indicator of a finders-keepers mentality.

After a while, I drove to Jennings Allen's house where I sat quietly for a time before going on to the house of Norman Christensen. Together, these three men were the first searchers into Davis Gulch. If I could just search these properties, something might turn up. It is a long shot, but from a distance of a half century, everything is a long shot. What if Everett's journal is hidden in one of these houses? I must find a way to get inside without attracting too much attention.

THE ESCALANTE SEARCHES

After pouring over the surviving documentation and after becoming intimately familiar with Davis Gulch and the surrounding area, I reluctantly concluded that the three quasi-official searches for Everett in the spring and summer of 1935 were totally inadequate. When the first search party from Escalante found Everett's burros and campsites in Davis Gulch, they did little else to find him. Who could blame them? They knew Everett was not coming back and the chance of locating his body was negligible. Time has proven them right.

My first clue that the searches lacked credibility came in a letter from H. Jennings Allen, leader of both Escalante expeditions, to Everett's parents, Christopher and Stella Ruess. He wrote, "Everett must have left this section and gone onto the Navajo reservation; he can't be anywhere on this side of the Colorado River alive because every inch has been searched."

Allen's statement troubled me. I knew that an army of searchers could spread out over the land and still have no guarantee of success. To think a handful of men on horseback could cover every inch of this jigsaw land was preposterous. I have personally gone over some of the same areas many times, and each time I've found previously undiscovered alcoves, caves, potholes, draws, overhangs, cracks in cliff lines, and crevasses where Everett could have fallen, taken sick, or sought refuge. Stockmen graze cattle here, and it is common for cows to be lost and never found. The sun-bleached bones of these creatures populate hidden places. I once found five steer skulls standing in a row at the base of a rock outcropping where someone had lined them up. The white bone against umber sandstone was dramatic. Curiously, the steer tines arced upward in a haunting, gravestone-like symmetry.

In all likelihood, Jennings Allen was trying to comfort the Ruess family, gently lowering their expectations and assuring them everything possible was done. While the revisionist's work is gleeful, even from a distance of nearly six decades, it is easy to see the searches for what they really were.

In June of 1935, after the State of Utah refused to spend its resources for an official enquiry, the Associated Civic Club of Southern Utah conducted its own search. While they found little new information, they did locate a white man who had camped the winter near Hole in the Rock, a distance of less than two miles from Davis Gulch. This man had not seen Everett.

Why didn't the first two search parties find this white man camping so near to Davis Gulch? Both search parties reported going to Hole in the Rock where they found Everett's boot prints in the sand. To make things even more troubling, the civic club search party did not get the name of the man they located. The identity of this white man haunts me. If I just knew who this white man was, it might help me discover the secret to what really happened to Everett.

Of the three searches, none included the area of Wilson Mesa, just east of the Colorado River. This would be analogous to searching one side of a neighborhood street for a lost child. Wilson Mesa would have been a likely place for Everett to explore while camping in Davis Gulch. There is also no evidence that Fifty Mile Mountain, the towering forest-topped escarpment west of Davis Gulch, received even a cursory search. Finally, no one ventured south of the Hole in the Rock trail into the maze-like territory below Fifty Mile Mountain or onto the foothills of Navajo Mountain.

Of all the confounding circumstances surrounding the searches, one of the most frustrating is the question of what the first searchers into Davis Gulch really found there. If Everett's camp outfit and equipment were found along with his burros and then divided up, the real picture of what happened was irreparably altered or destroyed entirely, leaving subsequent inquiries with little or no hope of piecing the puzzle together.

There are other theories about why Everett's pack outfit was never located. It is a strong possibility that Everett was killed by a renegade Navajo or cattle rustler intent on stealing his goods. This theory has merit but does not explain how the killer was able to make off with more than 200 pounds of equipment without using his burros to carry the load. This theory is also confounding because it is not likely that a thief willing to kill would leave behind his victim's most valuable possessions, the burros.

Another theory is that after Everett camped in Davis Gulch, he moved his campsite to another location but returned his burros to Davis Gulch where water and forage were plentiful. This theory also has merit, and if it is true, Everett's campsite may be sitting out in the desert as he left it. Perhaps Everett became sick and died or fell from a cliff and his remains and camp are out there right now waiting to be found. It is also a possibility that his camp equipment was subsequently found and taken by someone who had no idea of its importance and who never contacted the authorities.

All of this and more—which I will get to later—forced me to conclude that another search was necessary.

The next morning I drove east out of town. I was followed by two mud-caked four-wheel-drive trucks. They kept far back so as not to draw my attention. A few miles out of town they turned around at the entrance to a state-owned gravel bed and headed back toward town. I was happy to see them gone. In my rearview mirror, I watched as they suddenly dropped off the horizon and disappeared.

After gassing up in the town of Boulder, I drove out onto a side road named the Burr Trail. Until recently, the Burr Trail was one of the last premiere unimproved dirt roads in the West. Originally cut by ranchers wanting access to the wild unused canyons east of town for grazing and mining, the Burr Trail winds up and down canyons, over and around chocolate-, zinc-, and oxide-colored ridges, and strikes deep into the heart of remote and wild lands.

Within the first mile, the trail winds down a steep cliff face, glimpsing into a storybook-like canyon bottom. A year-round creek delicately laces its way between groves of cottonwood and is framed by towering canyon walls. Willows, red birch, long and short grasses, desert rice, tamarisks, and colorful desert flowers thrive along the creek's banks. Almost all desert wildlife depends upon this thin strip called the riparian zone. Like so much in the arid Southwest, the riparian zone's beauty is only equaled by its fragility.

The Burr crosses the creek once and then again before threading its way up the canyon. The Anasazi lived here and chronicled their lives on the canyon walls. About a mile farther, the creek vanishes into a side canyon and the trail climbs and narrows. The canyon walls close in and it appears the road cannot continue, when suddenly it serpentines to the right, then to the left, and climbs almost straight up.

From the canyon bottom, the trail climbs onto a narrow ridge top with deep blue and purple canyons falling away on either side. To the east, a vast errant canyon system rolls over itself again and again in the foreground. Above the confused canyons and twenty miles farther out, a series of cedar- and juniper-covered mesas dot the higher ground. To the southeast, colonies of elegant white monoliths shape the land like a beautiful woman's silhouette in repose, and still farther out, the multi-blue horizons fade into dust and eternity.

Pockets of profound silence can still be found along this road. This silence breaks on the ear like the tide of a great ocean. To the uninitiated, this silence must be broken. I have seen city people so unnerved by it that they have packed up and left—never to return. I have seen others act as if they have finally arrived back at a place they once knew but lost so very long ago.

The dominion of silence is shrinking. It can still be found, but one must walk and search the secret side canyons. Until I follow the path of the Ancient Ones over the far horizon, I will rejuvenate and renew myself in these clear, clean pools of silence and solitude.

At a certain place along the road, I turned onto what is left of an old mining road. Over the years, I've become secretive about my favorite camping places. I've made it my practice not to divulge too much information. Each person needs to make these discoveries on his or her own. The road passes through sagebrush flats and stands of cedar and juniper and then follows a wide floodplain. At first, the floodplain is several hundred yards wide, but over the course of a few miles it tapers down until it evolves into a narrow canyon with towering walls on either side. A quarter mile or so farther, I wheeled into a hidden side canyon. I have camped in this side canyon so many times, I feel a sense of ownership.

At a place where the canyon makes a large gentle U-turn, I parked and made camp. On a nearby hillside stands the sentinel of this place: a long-dead cedar tree twisting into the sky. I have often admired its beauty. It has welcomed me here many times, and I always marveled at its roots laying supine on top of the pink soil. This sentinel welcomes the passing of time. I was at home with the spirits here and with the inner and outer landscapes.

When the sun disappeared behind a line of cliffs, I walked out over hills, down gentle sloping canyons, and through open sage- and juniper-covered flats. I have walked this way before, meandering, looking for pottery shards and arrowheads. Long ago, Anasazi hunters searched for game here. They wore woven sandals and carried bows and arrows. From hilltop blinds they chipped flint and obsidian into arrowheads and waited for game. The discarded flint lies where they left it.

Once several years ago, as I walked a dry creek bed near there, I found a perfect stone spearhead. It was more than three inches long. I stood over the spearhead, admiring it for a long time before kneeling down to pick it up. A Navajo friend, Brigham Atene, once told me it was a good omen to find an object left by the Ancient Ones. "If you find an arrowhead," he said with the kind of straight face only Navajos can make, "it was left there for you by the ancestors. It is a talisman."

"Should I take these talismans when I find them, or leave them behind?"

"They are yours," he told me. "You would not find them if the Ancient Ones did not want you to have them. Take them when you find them."

At the time, this idea made sense to me, so I picked up the spearhead and examined it, holding it gently but firmly between my thumb and forefinger. It was exquisitely worked and felt smooth and glassy; I placed it in the palm of my other hand. Slowly, I closed my hand around its sharpened edges, and as I did, a deep sense of pride swept over me. Despite the odds against it, the Anasazi hunter and I had made a real connection. The talisman lay protected in the bed of my hand, and I was now part of its story.

As I walked alone this particular afternoon, musing about the spearhead I had found years earlier, my eyes caught sight of an object glistening in the sand about fifty feet away. Ah, another talisman, I said to myself, quickly making my way to the spot. As I drew near, I could see that the object was metal, garbage from an old mining camp, but I leaned down for closer examination anyway.

I picked up the piece of metal. It was a military-style dog-tag identification. It read: My name is Bask—I belong to Mark Taylor—539 S. 410 E. SLC, UT—801-511-0803. I couldn't believe it! This talisman was left years ago by my beloved dog, Bask. I turned in a circle and then called out, "Bask! Are you out there somewhere?" My question was absorbed into the silence. My mind traced back in time, and after some difficulty I recalled what had happened. Years ago, Bask and I walked this same area, and when we returned to camp his dog tag was missing from his collar. It happened the same day I found the spear tip.

Bask died of a heart attack a few years ago as I cradled him in my arms. He was my best friend and the most lionhearted creature I have ever known. He loved the deserts, and as I stood there rubbing my fingers across the stainless steel of his dog tag, the pain of his absence became unbearable.

I returned Bask's talisman to the earth and a strong sense of emptiness swept over me—Bask is still alive. He now resides on the landscape of my personal memory; he is one of the archaeological treasures within me. He is alive and ready to retrace any path we have shared or to strike out into the unknown. As long as I live my Basker-the-dog-faced-boy lives.

Unwittingly, I had been laying down an archaeological trail of my own. I had spent years searching for bits and pieces of Everett's passing and that of the Anasazi, but I had never considered that my quest—and that of my companions—was being documented by our debris.

Will future generations find us as fascinating as we find our predecessors? I suspect not.

NEAR MOAB, UTAH

L ater that night, I drove east along the river road outside of Moab, Utah, and camped on the wide sandy beach at a place called Big Bend. I knew this spot well and had base-camped there many times while exploring Canyonlands and Arches National Parks.

In the late 1960s, Big Bend was little known and locals called it Nude Beach. I often camped there with bohemian sun worshipers who had found their way to its sandy beaches from places the world over. Hidden from the roadway, we swam, sunbathed, and celebrated the silence. At night we stood naked around campfires and talked in whispers. It mattered little that we did not know one another; our golden nakedness assured us we were of the same tribe.

Over the years, I have come to enjoy arriving in the sandstone canyons after dark, and this particular night was no exception. I bailed out of my car, filled my lungs with clean air, pushed my hands into the small of my back, and arced to look at the Milky Way. Wow! Viewing the stars from the desert never fails to astound me.

Somewhere in the darkness, the Colorado River washed against its shoreline. The river called out to me, reminding me that I stood in the exact place where five years earlier my best friend, Mick Tripp, told me he loved me. I looked down, hoping to see my friend's footprints lying there in the dirt, but they were gone. Instead, my eyes followed the well-worn path to a small grove of gambel oak trees where I normally camp. Since my feet knew the path so well, I let them carry me to the oaks, then through an opening in a line of thick tamarisk trees and down to the river.

At the river's edge, I stood and faced upstream and then downstream. Starlight reflected off the water's surface making it appear placid and inviting, yet its roiling undertow frightened me, and I felt insignificant standing next to it. Not wanting to parade my intimidation, I plopped down in the sand and sat Indian style. I was the only human being for miles and not entirely welcomed by the river.

Just one month before Mick killed himself with a bullet to his heart, he and I escaped Salt Lake City and ran south into the desert. We camped at Big Bend and hiked the canyons. We hiked fast without stopping to rest, searching every alcove and hidden draw, every slope and amphitheater. We dropped stones into canyons and climbed escarpments. We were searching for something but had no idea what it was.

During a cavalier moment, as Mick and I stood surveying a fine prospect of sandstone formations, I told him that the face of every man, woman, and child who has ever lived can be found in the sandstone cliffs and formations.

"If that is so," he said, "then, I too, shall one day reside here."

Since Mick's death, I have seen him here three times. The first time, I was watching a magnificent sunset above Arch Canyon when out on the serrated horizon, the silhouette of his face appeared. It was perfect to a minute detail. The next time, I was atop Grandview Point in Canyonlands when his face took shape in the morning shadow of Junction Butte below me, moving across an expanse of sagebrush flats until it twisted, contorted, and became unrecognizable. The last time I saw Mick's face, it was rendered on a palette of rain-soaked, vermilion-colored Kayenta sandstone above Davis Gulch where Everett disappeared.

From the beach, I searched the surrounding cliffs, hoping the starlight might catch Mick there. He was out there somewhere, I told myself, along with all the others—but tonight they remained hidden.

I became restless sitting on the beach, so I moved to the grove of gambel oaks where Mick had unrolled his sleeping bag for the very last time. The night was liquid, and I couldn't shake my fear of the river. I was convinced Mick wanted to live. Standing next to some nearby rocks, he had told me of his plan to buy a new Harley Davidson motorcycle.

On his last night in the desert, Mick sat against the very tree where I sat.

"Life and death come face to face in the desert," he told me. "Our lives have little consequence in view of the 300 million years of history around us here. When I am gone my friend, this is where you will find me."

It has been five years since Mick took his leave, and I honor him more with each passing season. Strange as it may sound, I have kept my friend alive by incorporating his voice and point of view into the world of my internal dialogues. He now advocates at the round table of my soul, speaking to me if he has something to say, and if I query him, he is always there to answer.

"Hey, Mick!" I shouted out into the unattached darkness, "What am I lookin' at on the other side, Bro?"

From the river below came his reply, "Taylor, the only thing waiting for you is an icy black river of night!"

There was a moment of silence, then he cut loose with a loud horse laugh, the one I hated when he was alive.

Sometime after the Hopi wind god, Yaponcha, swept down the canyon in search of nocturnes, I fell soundly asleep. It was not my nature to sleep late, but I was exhausted and did not stir until the sun reached me in the canyon bottom.

Throughout the canyons of the Colorado River Plateau, the river creates a rich riparian strip along its banks where vegetation and wildlife flourish. At Big Bend, tamarisk bushes dominate the river banks and narrow alluvial plain. Introduced hundreds of years ago by the Spanish to the American Southwest, the prolific tamarisk has choked out the beautiful red-river birch thickets that once prospered here, unchallenged for eons.

From my camp I followed a coyote trail to the base of a nearby thousand-foot escarpment. In and among the rocks grew desert grasses, blooming bushes, and wildflowers. Pink, red, and orange Indian paintbrush reached up to meet the sky. It was difficult to imagine how anyone could call this land a desert. At the foot of the cliff's debris-strewn talus slope, colonies of hedgehog and prickly pear cactus blossomed. Their large waxy yellow and lavender flowers would not survive the hottest part of the day. Communities of orange globe mallow and scarlet bugler added delicacy to the teetering boulders and rock jumble.

At a sandbar back near camp, I drank coffee and surveyed the footprints of Big Bend's nocturnal residents. While I slept, fox, kangaroo rats, ringtailed cats (part of the raccoon family), coyotes, chipmunks, and mice went about their daily routines. The white sand was so fine that even the smallest creature's tracks were imprinted in exquisite detail. Whiptail lizard trails crisscrossed the sand and lay among the prints of heavy blue-black beetles and large red ants.

I was desperate for the peace and quiet of this land, and it felt damned good to be there. When I reached a certain point along the road into this country, a strange and wonderful transformation began within me. Inside my abdominal cavity, all my organs seemed to relax and softly nestle among each other. A genuine sense of goodwill replaced the empty anxiety of my petty existence. This land was the only true safe haven I had ever known. Though it is infinite in its configuration, from its lofty cliffs and deep canyons to the intimacy of every meter of sand, I discovered a kind of uniformity of uniqueness there, even a place for me in this scheme. My transformation began the moment I arrived at Big Bend. It would take days to decompress from the writing assignment I had just completed.

Transformation from frenetic American modernism to solitude was never easy for me and had a surreal, dream-like quality. This particular transformation was especially important to me because I had just returned from a six-month undercover investigation of Jimmy Swaggart and his Assembly of God World Ministry in Baton Rouge, Louisiana. For the next number of days (I didn't know how many), I would forget the termite mound I left behind. I planned to take up Everett's trail again to see if I could see what he saw and experience what he might have experienced. My first stop would be at Hap Marshall's, an eighty-five-year-old hermit who lived out in the wilderness with his two dogs and a dozen or so cats.

As I departed Big Bend, I was happy that it remained much the way it was when Mick and I first discovered it. Because of its proximity to Moab, I knew that Big Bend's days as it is now, as nature created it, were numbered. One day, Big Bend would be home to RVs, asphalt pads, discarded disposable diapers, and all the other trail cairns our society uses to mark its passing.

After buying supplies at the City Market in Moab, I settled in for the hour's drive south to Hap Marshall's run-down shack. I felt good; the majesty of this place enveloped me. Like Everett, Hap came from the city in the 1920s, fell in love with the country, and stayed. Over the last fifty years, Hap had worked as a prospector, a uranium miner, and a carpenter. Except for his dogs and cats, Hap lived alone at the end of a rutted four-wheel-drive road. The road once continued past his place to a long-played-out uranium mine, but it had been reclaimed by nature and only telltale signs of its existence remained.

It was never Hap's intention to become a hermit. "When the red sand gets into your blood," he once told me, "there's nothing you can do about it." At his age, Hap's friends were dead, living in nursing homes, or had simply disappeared. He lost track of his family years ago, and he lived alone, tending to his canine and feline family and waiting for something to happen.

I had visited Hap many times over the last few years. When he saw my car coming down the dirt road, he always walked out to greet me, offering a strong handshake. Then he usually inquired about any spare canned goods he might share with his pets. We sat outside in the shade, knocking down beers while he told me stories of his time in the desert. Hap was one of the last real desert rats of Everett's generation who was still alive. He even met Everett once:

> *"I knew he wouldn't make it, and I'll be damned if I know what all the fuss is about. . . . Let's see, it must have been in the early thirties, and I was working on a ranch outside of Flagstaff*

when up comes this baby-faced kid and his dog. He rode atop a palomino pony and asked the rancher—Brewer was his name—if there was any work he could do for food. Well, ol' Brewer put him to work choppin' wood. It was a pitiful sight, the boy had never chopped wood before. I remember thinkin' he needed to put more meat on his bones.

"Anyway, he was a good sort o' kid, polite, city-like and we all liked him. . . . I still don't know what all the fuss is about. The kid was one of hundreds who got the desert bug and took up living in the Moki ruins. The only thing I can see that's so special about him is that he succeeded in getting himself lost or killed. That don't seem to be such a great accomplishment to me."

Hap's memory delighted me. Sitting next to him made me feel closer to Everett. I can't help but wonder that if Everett had survived whether he might have ended up out here alone just like Hap. Once, after an afternoon drinking beer and talking about the land, Hap turned to me and said, "You know, you remind me of Everett a little. You have that same friendly way and you ask the same stupid questions he asked."

Hap told me there was more, something else he remembered about Everett, but he couldn't bring it to mind. He got up and went into his shack; when he returned he was shaking his head. "Next time you come by, I'll be wanting to show you something."

Hap's generation was the second of European descent to fall in love with this spectacular country. Like the Anasazi before the Europeans, when they die out, their wisdom will be lost forever.

Every time I start down the dirt road leading to Hap's place, I cannot help but wonder if I will be the one to find him dead. I imagine seeing his starving dogs, limping out to meet me. From the mere look of them, I'll know Hap is gone. Luckily, this bleak scenario has yet to play out, but this time as I pulled into his yard, he did not come out to greet me. I got out of my vehicle and waited for his dogs to appear from behind the house, barking and fussing. The dogs were fat and sassy, reassuring me that everything was all right.

I searched for Hap but could not find him, so I walked into the sagebrush chaparral behind the house, calling out to him though he is totally deaf. I climbed a nearby sandstone formation and scanned the horizon for movement. I circled his property. Nothing. Finally, I wrote a note, fed his animals, and placed a box of canned goods and beer inside his doorway. I reluctantly drove back to the highway.

Two hours later in Blanding, Utah, as I gassed up for a side trip to Grand Gulch, I spotted Anasazi rock-art artist Joe Pachek crossing Main Street.

Pachek was walking in the direction of his house a few blocks away. His head was lowered, and he appeared to be immersed in thought. I quickly paid for the gas and drove to his house, hoping to catch him before he arrived. I have known Pachek for several years and prefer talking to him outdoors.

Pachek was ill-at-ease indoors. By contrast, outdoors he smiled more often and seemed at ease. Inside, he paced and was sullen. Outside, he rested easily upon the ground and opened up. Pachek embodied the white wild man Victorian America attempted to discard many generations ago in favor of the outward appearance of civility. He was short, muscular, lean, and preferred wearing boots and hiking shorts. His deep tan accentuated his well-defined muscles, and his blonde hair flowed freely from his shoulders down over his back like rain off the cliffs.

I pulled up just as Joe was unlocking the front door to his house.

"Marcus!" he called out, "back from Swaggart-land? Come on in."

"No way," I said. "I've been stuck inside for nearly six months. Let's sit on the porch."

Without a word, Pachek sprawled on the hardened dirt where lawn once grew. I sat on the cement steps as we caught up on each other's life. It felt good sharing his company, but after a while Joe fell silent, and it was easy to see something was wrong. Joe stared past me to the horizon west of town. He began to brood.

"Everything okay, Joe?"

"Yes."

After a few quiet moments, he said, "No, I guess something is the matter. I feel my art calling to me. Do you ever feel that way?"

"Do I hear voices?" I asked.

"No, not exactly. What I mean is, does your art call to you in a spiritual way?"

I didn't know what to say. I felt something important and exciting was about to happen. "I'm not entirely sure of what you're talking about."

"Around back," he said nodding his head and jumping to his feet.

Sitting in Pachek's backyard was a stunning, larger-than-life, sandstone-colored, stylized cement sculpture of an antelope. The piece had long swept-back horns, making a simple four-foot arc. Its legs were elegant and narrow, sculpted in full stride. The torso was also arced in such a way that the entire piece seemed in flight. Although constructed of cement, the sculpture was anything but bulky or heavy. It possessed a lean, sleek, and even wild quality—the energy of Art Deco combined with expressionist imagery. The combination was incongruous yet perfect.

Pachek had modeled the piece from an Anasazi pictograph in Grand Gulch. I knew at first glance that it was museum quality; it would live much longer than its creator.

"Does it speak to you?" he asked, embarrassed.

"It's fabulous, Joe. Truly. If it flew off right now, I would not be one bit more impressed."

"It's not mine," he said. "The artist who designed it died hundreds of years ago. I only sculpted it from his design. Actually, though, my hands made it." He held out his large hands and turned them over and over. We stood and gazed at them for a long time.

"Maybe so, Joe," I said, "but at the very least, I believe it's a collaborative work. The artist and you. Without you, this piece wouldn't exist."

"Yes! Yes. Right," he said, cocking his head to the left and closing one eye. "You're right. A collaboration!" He was excited by what I'd said, and that made me feel good.

We did not speak for a long time; instead, we slowly circled the antelope in a reverent and ritual-like way.

Pachek had come to this land from the city a decade ago without fanfare or contradiction. Like young Everett, Pachek belonged to this geography, and it mattered little where his journey had begun or even what had happened to him before he arrived. Unlike Everett, Pachek belonged to the spirit of the Anasazi. At age thirty-seven, he was dedicated to empowering the spiritual energy of the Ancient Ones who once shared this land.

The world of art has not let Pachek's work go unappreciated. Art galleries want to exhibit and sell his work. Natural history museums rearrange their exhibition schedules to display his work. Yet even with all the attention, Pachek remains impoverished. To Joe, his art is an expression of faith, a salute to the energy of the people who once lived there. He refuses to sell his work, saying, "It is a mistake to sell my work; they [the Anasazi] do not want me to."

"Joe," I finally asked, "what does this piece say to you?"

"It says that I am in love with a woman. I have never felt this way before. My hands made it for her."

I left Pachek standing in his backyard and drove south from Blanding to Highway 95, then west onto Cedar Mesa and to Grand Gulch. My plan was to explore the little-known Green Mask Cave.

Starting about the time of Jesus Christ, Grand Gulch was inhabited on and off for long periods by many generations of Anasazi and other pre-Columbian natives. According to the journals of John Wetherill, one of the first white men into the gulch, it appeared that the last inhabitants of the gulch had left quickly, leaving everything behind. The canyon was a perfect mosaic of who the Anasazi had been. Unfortunately, successive generations of pothunters and grave robbers have destroyed much of this picture.

From my car, I hiked through the beautiful cedar and juniper forest until the trail dropped into the gulch. There, I walked the dry riverbed along its meandering route until late afternoon. Cliff dwellings, granaries, and pictographs were everywhere. At a place where two canyons intersected the main gulch, I stopped and called out to my dog, Bask. Bask's name rolled off the canyon walls and returned to me from three directions. The Cheyenne Indians teach that when loved ones die, it is important to continue speaking their names aloud. If you do not do this, your tongue will swell up, you will go crazy, and then you will die.

I called out Everett's name, then Mick's name, and then the names of all the others. I called out their names quickly and they returned to me just as quickly, washing over me one after another like the summer wind's soft caress. When the last echo died away, a deep silence and sadness enveloped me. I stood my ground and called out their names again.

Sunset comes early in the deep canyon, and when the last rays of light gave way to the dusk, I climbed a steep embankment to a cliff dwelling perched high above the canyon floor. The sun still bathed the ruin in golden light, allowing me to find pottery shards and ancient corncobs with the markings of human teeth. I placed my mat and sleeping bag in the main room of the ruin and rested. The original resident would have slept right here, I said to myself, and fell off to sleep. I awoke to the blue-grey disc of Jupiter winking at me through the south window. From the doorway, the red planet Mars crowned the canyon rim like a jewel at the center of a tiara.

My sleep was fitful, and I was awakened many times. I was not alone there, I thought. I moved outside under the stars, but I could not shake the feeling that I did not belong there. Long before the sun tipped down into the canyon, I was miles away, standing at the entrance of the Green Mask Cave.

The mystery of the cave remains largely unknown and unexplained but offers controversial glimpses into who the Anasazi were and what may have happened to them. While most anthropologists and archaeologists believe the Anasazi were agrarian and nonviolent, the mummies and bones found in the cave tell another story. Many believe the mummies found in the cave died in sacrificial rituals. Some possessed the look of excruciating pain on their faces; others were decapitated and their heads were placed inside their abdominal cavity. Some had their arms and legs amputated and then sewn back in the wrong places. Most controversial of the discoveries at the cave were the neatly piled human bones bearing the markings of human teeth.

Were the Anasazi cannibals, or did a drought and starvation force them to eat human flesh?

Above the cave's entrance was a large unique pictograph. The pictograph represents a face with two green slashes running horizontally through it. The Anasazi left thousands of pictographs and petroglyphs behind, and most have an easily identifiable style and design, yet the three known Green Masks are unlike any of them. The design of the mask found here is oval and appears African; it also possesses a highly unusual overlay of green pigmentation. The two other green mask pictographs are located at places of great religious and societal significance. One is in Chaco Canyon at the site of the great Anasazi city of Chaco. The other is located on the sacred three-fingered mesas of the Hopi Indians. These two sites have not been excavated, and the masks' significance, if any, remains a mystery.

As I stood at the entrance to the cave examining the mask, a wave of anxiety rushed over me. My original plan was to camp at the cave for two days, but as I stood there I suddenly changed my mind. I felt I should leave immediately. I moved off a few steps, then stopped. No, I told myself, stay long enough to explore the cave and the surrounding area.

Just as I was about to enter the cave, I saw a piece of bone partially unearthed and lying near the entryway. It was a human jawbone. I couldn't believe my good luck; I dropped to my knees and began frantically digging into the bronze soil with my bare hands. A few minutes later, sweat beaded my forearms and brow; the ground was so hard I could go no further. I ripped my shirt off, found a flat rock, and began enlarging my excavation.

Generations of pothunters have come and gone before me. Grave robbers have dug into burial mounds, taking the jewelry and religious icons and discarding the human remains. It was not my intention to follow in the path of their desecration. I was not there to disturb anyone's final resting place. I would never take the jawbone with me, but for a few minutes as I dug deeper and deeper, I experienced what can be best described as pothunter's fever. To the spirits of the canyon it must have appeared that I was just another desecrator. The entire canyon system was, in fact, a sacred burial ground where thousands of souls were interred.

When I tired and leaned back against the Green Mask entryway to rest, the canyon seemed hostile and abrasive. The broken rock looked war-like; the cedars on the cliff ledges above dipped and rolled in the wind like warriors catching first sight of an enemy. Shapes darted behind rocks. I thought I heard dogs barking, men shouting, and women sobbing.

I have offended the spirits who reside in the canyon, I thought. These spirits are known by the Hopi Indians as *Kaa*, meaning "the spirit born into the individual who lives side by side through life, then continues living on after the individual dies to protect the burial mound."

I suddenly felt dizzy and knew that if I stood I might fall, so I sat there and cowered. I decided to plead my case to the spirits. Sitting Indian style, I squared my shoulders and spoke, "I have worked to protect your land," I began, "I honor you and your ancestors. I am sorry for digging in your Earth."

I did not have long to wait for my answer. A cold wind rushed out of the cave and swirled around me. The hair on the back of my neck bristled, and shivers raced up and down my spine.

On my hands and knees, I crawled to the hole, gingerly placed the jaw-bone in the bottom, and frantically filled it in. I then stumbled down the hill to the creek bed and hiked out of the canyon, trying not to look to my right or left but, instead, focusing on every step in front of me. I did not stop to rest until I reached my car on Cedar Mesa above.

From Cedar Mesa I drove south to Mexican Hat, straddling the Utah-Arizona border at the north end of Monument Valley. I rented a run-down room at the Trading Post Motel. It was refreshing to take a shower, sleep in a bed, and still be able to walk outside and see crows floating above my beloved desert.

The next morning, I started out for Kayenta, hoping to locate the family of famed Navajo tracker, Dougi, and others who knew Everett. I will travel the path Everett took, following his footprints across the face of the land just as he did for the last eight months of his life. On the western horizon, I could see Navajo Mountain more than fifty miles away.

The Navajo, or *Dineh*, as they call themselves, meaning "the People," have lived in the Four Corners area since the 1600s when Spanish conquistadors drove them north out of Mexico. For hundreds of years, the nomadic Navajo made pilgrimages to Navajo Mountain where they collected herbs and prayed. No one lived on the mountain because it was sacred. Many Navajo gods are said to reside there. Even today, the magic of the mountain is so strong that traditionalists will not venture out after dark because they fear they will never return.

The first Dineh to live on the mountain's foothills did so after escaping the United States Cavalry in 1863 when Washington decided that all natives in what is now northern Arizona and New Mexico might be a threat and ordered they be rounded up and marched to Bosque Redondo, the name natives gave to the newly built Fort Sumner. Led by the explorer and then United States Cavalry captain, Kit Carson, nearly 4,500 Dineh and 2,000 Mescalaro Apache were forced from their homes. Carson and his men destroyed their farm fields, orchards, villages; they poisoned water holes and slaughtered all their livestock. Some Dineh fought back but were no match for the well-armed military. More than 400 people were killed resisting and another 400 were shot outright along the 300-mile trail for not being able to keep up, most of them were women, old people, and small children.

Those who survived the nightmarish trek to Bosque Redondo were forced to live outside with no shelter, little food, and almost no water. Hundreds died from starvation or typhoid when unscrupulous white Indian agents distributed typhoid-infected blankets as protection from the cold winter wind. After four years of living outside, those who survived were allowed to return to their homes. Today, the Dineh call this dark episode in the tribe's history The Long March. While more than 100 years have past, the Dineh have not forgotten the inhumane treatment they received at the hands of the new Americans.

One band of Dineh who managed to escape The Long March took refuge on Navajo Mountain and lived there in isolation for more than a generation. No one, including their fellow Dineh, knew they were there. Most of the residents of Navajo Mountain today are descendants of its first residents. They consider themselves purer and perhaps wilder than the other Navajo clans.

Nearing Kayenta, I saw smoke snakes to my left, rising from hogans built on the desolate hills outside town.

"What do you expect to find here?" Mick asked from the round table.

"I don't know."

Silence.

"Taylor, you are a fool!"

"Though the cloth is worn, my friend, I will pursue every thread until the secret of what Everett found here is mine."

EVERETT IN KAYENTA, ARIZONA

Kayenta, Arizona, is a Navajo town, and if one looks past the convenience stores, fast-food eateries, and self-service gas stations, it is easy to imagine what it might have looked like during Everett's time.

Before Everett returned to Kayenta and his beloved desert in the spring of 1934 to begin what was to be the last leg of his journey, he spent the winter in San Francisco, living the life of an artist. From his cheap boardinghouse room on Broadway Street, Everett experienced the swell and clash of creative life, testing himself in the dark and tumultuous ocean of artists.

With only pennies in his pocket, Everett walked the streets in search of beauty and adventure. When he wasn't feasting on the city's museums, music, and performing arts, he was holed up in his room working diligently on his sketches and designs. At age nineteen, Everett was far ahead of his contemporaries. He appreciated philosophy and possessed a deep love for beauty and art. His appreciation of philosophy came from Christopher, his father, a graduate of the Harvard Divinity School.

From his father, Everett was given the wings for intellectual and spiritual flight. Everett understood that these wings do not come fully formed; one must be patient and dedicated to working hard. Just as important, he seemed to know that flight requires gravity to make it work. From his mother, Stella, an accomplished artist and art educator, he was given an acute sense of beauty and a special understanding of its soulful imagery. She imparted on him the importance of looking deep inside himself and trusting the images and feelings he found there. Stella showed her beloved son ways to express these images and feelings, utilizing nature as his vocabulary.

Many people called at the Ruess house when Everett was a child. It was not unusual to find artists, writers, philosophers, neighbors, and even community leaders engaged in lively discussions around the dining-room table. Everett became a skilled communicator, developing his own point of view and individual brand of wit. At the same time, he was enthralled by the mystery of life and especially the path his own life would follow.

Because of this enriched family environment, Everett did not hesitate to seek out people he wanted to know and to introduce himself. Soon after arriving in San Francisco, he made the acquaintance of Ansel Adams. One day Everett just showed up at Adam's studio. Adams was so impressed with Everett's block prints that he traded one of his better photographs for one of Everett's better prints. The same thing happened at the house of painter Maynard Dixon and wife, photographer Dorothea Lange. One day they heard a knock on the door, and when they opened it, there stood Everett, hat in hand. They were so taken by this enthusiastic young man, they invited him to live with them. Lange sensed something special in Everett and saw to furthering his artistic instruction, taking him to concerts and introducing him to people and many new ideas.

During an earlier visit in 1931, Everett had made the acquaintance of the famed photographer Edward Weston, who also invited him to stay at his house. Weston introduced Everett to his minimalist's lifestyle and view of the world. The wisdom of great artists is best glimpsed when listening to their survival stories. No doubt Everett heard his share during the winter of 1933–34 in San Francisco. Usually at the heart of these stories is a central theme: we are all works in progress; it takes time and many mistakes to make an artist.

Everett already had a plan for developing his abilities and talents long before arriving in San Francisco. He knew it was going to take time. Here is an excerpt from a letter written to his dear friend Bill, from the Arizona desert in 1931: "My plan is to amble about the southwest with donkeys for a couple of years more, gathering plenty of material and mastering watercolor technique—then to get some windfall so I can work with oils and do things on a larger scale, perfect my field studies and then do something with what I have."

In San Francisco, Everett worked feverishly on his visual art and writing, yet his work was met with a confusing mixture of praise, disdain, and indifference. Like most young artists, Everett's work ranged from painfully naive to quite accomplished. Paul Elder, owner of the most influential art gallery in the city, took Everett's block prints on consignment—a very unusual circumstance for a young artist—but when Everett returned sometime later, hoping for a payday, Elder had not even taken the time to hang his work.

Today, Everett's block prints are valuable and cherished by those who love the land. Part of their attraction has to do with his disappearance, but at the same time his work possesses beauty and eloquence. Many of his block prints exhibit a style, technique, and composition usually attributed to older, more experienced artists. Some of this can be traced to Stella Ruess who was an accomplished block-print artist, but Everett learned early to be fiercely independent and exhibited a unique vision of his own. Still, his mother influenced his art and artistic perspective profoundly. When Everett was ten, Stella sent him by train from the family home in Valparaiso, Indiana, to study art at the Chicago Art Institute every Saturday. When the family moved to Los Angeles in 1928, Stella enrolled him in classes at the Otis Art School.

While San Francisco suffered a cold heavy fog during the winter of 1933, much of the world was hot with turmoil. The worldwide depression had deepened and threatened to collapse world economic order. Fascism took root in Europe. Suspicion and resentment of those who prospered ripened everywhere. In America, an entire generation of young men was swept up by the concussive wind of the rails and carried off like worthless chaff over the barren countryside.

Everett was not exempt from the oily political discussions of the day. He wrote about attending political speeches by communists and the International Workers of the World. He indulged in politically charged debates with activists. In a letter to his father dated December 13, he explained,

> . . . my communist friends were firing it at me when I told them that beauty and friendship were all I asked of life. I am not unconcerned with the crisis of our civilization, but the way of the agitator, the social leader, and the politician is not my way. It is not in my nature to deal with masses of people and be an organizer, and I don't propose to make any fundamental changes in my nature. I couldn't change that anyway.

At the same time, Everett could neither brush off the nascent ache of city life nor his own growing self-conscious preoccupations with his own value. As the winter deepened, Everett's moods darkened and his desire to return to the wilderness grew, as did his need to express his true feelings. In the same letter, he hinted about his need to express his innermost feeling:

> If more people felt that fineness was hoped for from them, and would not be scorned, they would respond and the world would be more beautiful. As it is, many people are ashamed of deep feelings when they have them, and always try to hide them. Don't you think that is true?

Not surprisingly, Everett's stay in San Francisco was punctuated by periods of creative paralysis. Artistic paralysis can be saline: its corrosive salts eat away at the soft and tender underside of dreams and ideals. For Everett, this inability to work and his need to express it is glimpsed in a letter written to his brother, Waldo, a few weeks later and dated December 22:

Dear Waldo,

I did not answer your letters earlier because most of the time I have been in a very restive, unstable mood, and did not feel like writing. I feel particularly that way tonight, but father remarked that you were hurt by my silence.

Perhaps, as someone said the other day, it is just because I am nineteen and sensitive, but it is small consolation to be told that. I have been discovering new moods, new lows, new and disturbing variations in myself and my feeling for individuals and people as a whole.

On the other hand, there is a lot of fun in me yet, and I have had some unusually gay times that were not feverishly so. But for the most part there has been an undercurrent of resentment or unrest.

After various turnings, twistings and recoils, I still have not been able to find any proper outlet for my feelings. Perhaps there is none and perhaps it is necessary for my feelings to die of weariness and refusal.

I won't apologize for my emotions because I don't feel completely responsible. I can trace certain reactions in them when I am analytic, but I do not care to now. I don't expect you to understand them any more than anyone else, nor would it matter much if you did, because it seems to be up to me.

Don't let my straying from normalcy disturb you; doubtless it is part of a somewhat symmetrical scheme which I seem to see dimly.

Your brother Everett

The symmetry of Everett's return to the desert in April 1934 outlined a final turning away from the expectations the world demanded of him. By choosing to become a wanderer, Everett was really defining what he was not. Plunging into the unknown, he cleansed himself of society's expectations and, in a way, transformed himself into a deeper, more complete, and more fulfilled person.

Everett gained perspective and depth in San Francisco, and these invaluable tools allowed him to compare and contrast the frenetic, almost manic excitement of the city with the solace of the quiet open spaces of the wilds. Shortly after his arrival back in Arizona, he wrote to a friend, Frances, in San Francisco: "I had many gloriously beautiful experiences (in the city), as well as the wild and intense adventures which seemed to come without my searching. I do not know if I shall ever return to the cities again, but I cannot complain that I found them empty of beauty."

The contrast between San Francisco and the land allowed Everett to better understand just how much he loved nature. He could not deny the intoxicating allure of the city, but the serenity of the desert assured him he was home. The Roman emperors and caesars understood the connection we all have to the land, especially the artists and poets. When Caesar was angry with an unflattering poet or when he disliked a work of art, he punished its creator by exiling him. Separation from one's homeland was thought to be the most excruciating punishment imaginable, even worse than death. Ovid, the great Roman poet who gave us the beautiful and self-absorbed Narcissus, wrote an epic poem during his exile, hoping Caesar would pardon him after reading of his pain and sorrow. Unfortunately, Ovid's plan did not work and he withered away, dying without ever returning home.

Back on the land, Everett accepted that a piece of the sky and a piece of the earth was buried within him. He followed his feelings and intuitions rather than arguing against them. Solitude is a poetry, and it reminds us to listen to our own poetry. Everyday, we write out the lines of our lives but seldom stop to listen to them. Once again, Everett walked ahead of his contemporaries.

KAYENTA, ARIZONA

After being out on the land—even if just for a few days—I find it difficult to venture back into town. Like Everett, I long for the experience of sanctuary and solace to continue unbroken. When I'm out in the wild, I often think that one day I, too, shall never return to the city.

Over the years, I have visited Kayenta many times, and as I drove slowly through town this time, I realized I have never felt at ease there. Kayenta is one of those places where an uncertain dominant society finds itself on the land of a reluctant and proud subordinate society. The American and the Native American cultures meet and comingle here for the sake of commerce, yet a palpable sense of tension hangs in the air.

Historically, white explorers and adventurers used Kayenta as a jumping-off point into the vast, untamed wild lands surrounding it. Everett spent several months there during the early 1930s, exploring Monument Valley and making friends among the Navajo. I, too, have a good friend who lives nearby. He has helped with my search for Everett. His name is Brigham Joseph Atene. I had not seen Brigham in a long time. We first met in 1986 when I was in Kayenta covering the Hopi-Navajo land dispute for a national magazine. He had just returned to the reservation after being away for many years.

Brigham and I planned to meet at the Kayenta 7-11 store and then travel out onto Big Mountain where he had located an old medicine man who remembered Everett. When I pulled into the 7-11 parking lot, Brigham had not arrived yet, so I parked and waited. It was in this very parking lot that Brigham and I had met and become friends.

At the time, I had just spent several days camping at Big Mountain with 200 fired-up Navajo activists and their supporters from the American Indian Movement (AIM). These angry men were itching for a fight with the Bureau of Indian Affairs (BIA) and the Arizona National Guard after threats were made to forcefully remove them from Big Mountain if they did not leave by the appointed date, July 7, one week away. While the activists were itching for a fight, I was itching for a cold Coke and a telephone, so I left the mountain and drove to Kayenta where I dialed up people who might help me find Everett's footprints here. It was while I was making telephone calls that Brigham and I met. I will never forget that night.

"Spare change?" A deep voice asked from the sidewalk behind me.

I turned to find a buffalo-sized Navajo man, Brigham Joseph Atene, standing before me. His oversized army-style camouflage jacket could barely accommodate his tremendous shoulders and fifty-gallon-barrel girth. An alcohol-induced stupor deadened his eyes.

"Yutahey," he said slowly. Brigham was unsteady and wavered like a great tree in the wind.

I retrieved the contents of my front pocket and dropped it into his grizzly-bear-sized hand. Along with some quarters, dimes, and nickels were several gum wrappers and pieces of wadded-up wastepaper. Brigham patiently picked out the trash from among the coins and dropped it to the ground. A garbage can was five feet away. When he was finished, he turned and walked away without saying a word.

A few minutes later a shadow was cast down over me. He was back.

"Spare change?" He was standing at attention, like a military man. "Yutahey," he said clearly. His voice clear and resonant.

"I gave you all my change," I said.

"Not enough."

"For what?"

"Mad Dog." He stared at his open hand as though it would tell the story. The coins lying there looked like miniature counterfeits.

"No more change," I answered, resolutely.

"Spare change?" he said again.

Suddenly, I felt anxious. I am an alien on foreign soil, I thought. Navajo land is a sovereign nation. I am a visitor here. My energy may not be wanted here. My American-ness may not be appreciated.

"Look," Brigham said in perfect English, "I am drunk. I will be sober tomorrow. I have come from the city. San Francisco. I am alone." His huge chest rose and fell with sadness.

"You don't live here?" I asked.

"It was my home once, long ago. I am here because my grandmother is dying," he paused as if trying to control his emotion. "I will go to her place tomorrow. Tonight, I am afraid to go home." He pulled the long hair away from his face and looked down at me.

I was speechless.

"I will get sober tomorrow," he said again. "Help me buy some hootch. I will share it with you."

"Thanks," I said, "but no thanks. I'm waiting for someone." Pulling my wallet from my back pocket, I asked, "How much for a bottle of Mad Dog?"

"I knew you was a good man!" he said, relieved. He then reached out to grasp my shoulder in a gesture of goodwill but instead lost his balance and fell on me. For several moments we danced around in a circle, struggling to stay afoot. He smelled of bitter layers of sweat, alcohol, and motor oil.

Brigham disappeared into the store; when he reappeared he was carrying a brown paper bag pushed against his midsection, like a fullback protecting a football. Turning to me, he raised the bottle over his head, hollered something, and disappeared around the corner.

A few minutes later he was back again. He had circled around the back of the building and was standing at its corner. He nodded at me.

"What?" I asked impatiently.

"Come over here."

"You come over here," I said.

He made a few tentative steps forward; he was accustomed to doing what white men told him. Nodding to the bottle in his hand and then to the street, he said, "Federales."

For the very first time Brigham really saw me. "You a Vietnam vet?" he asked, spraying me with wine and spit.

"Aren't we all?" I snapped a sharp salute.

He lifted the bottle out and away from his body, arcing it in a circle. "We are all veterans of this Vietnam, and of this heartless motherfucking world!"

He stood at attention and saluted me. "Corporal Brigham Joseph Atene. Reporting for duty, sir."

"At ease, soldier," I said. Something occurred to me. Once, I had seen Atene's silhouette, his torso, chest, and face chiseled in a sandstone cliff. It was far out in the wilderness, and I had forgotten all about it.

"Eighty-second Airborne. Two tours in Nam. The A Shua Valley." He saluted again, this time with the bottle to his lips. He held the bottle out and I grasped it. I put it to my lips and took several long pulls.

"Holy sweet mother of pearl!"

"We can't talk here," Atene said, taking the bottle quickly away from me. "Around back."

Behind the store, four young Navajos were sitting on the hardened, oil-soaked ground. Thousands of sharp pieces of green, brown, and clear glass from broken wine bottles surrounded them. Atene and I sat on a mound of dirt and talked. Night fell and occasionally the errant headlights of a car out on the highway caught the shards of glass and transformed them into sparkling jewels.

"I took the scalps of some gooks," Brigham told me. "It made me go crazy. The doctors said it was battle fatigue or Agent Orange, but I took the spirits from these men and have been paying for it ever since."

One of the young men nearby stood, took the bottle from Brigham, and drank from it. He then performed a flawless Michael Jackson moonwalk across the carpet of glass to his friends, who were waiting at attention. They helped themselves until the bottle was finished off.

I gave Corporal Brigham Joseph Atene enough money for two more bottles, and when he returned he continued telling his story. Brigham was raised outside of Window Rock where his father had been a uranium miner until he became sick and died. When the family finally learned he died of radiation poisoning, there was nothing they could do.

"He wasted away in our hogan," Brigham said. "He was a true patriot, but he was never accepted by the country he gave his life to protect."

Atene broke down and cried. He covered his face and rocked back and forth, then side to side. His pain was hard to watch. I wanted to put my arm around him to give him comfort, but I did not.

After awhile, Atene went on with his story. He said that not long after his father died, his mother died too, and he and his sisters were sent off to the Indian School in Brigham City, Utah. His sisters married Mormons and he was drafted into the army. In the army, he learned about drugs and alcohol. When he returned from Vietnam, his sisters denied him; their new lives did not include room for a drunk. Since then, Brigham had lived in exile, separated from his family and from the country that betrayed him. He was now back on the reservation for the first time in years because his grandmother was very ill.

The four young Navajos joined us. We passed the third bottle of Mad

Dog around the circle and Atene continued his story. Just as he was telling us about his Uncle Larry, who was a code talker in WWII—a name given to Navajos who befuddled the Japanese radio transmission code breakers by speaking Navajo—and who had been killed by stepping on a land mine shortly after the end of the war, one of the young Navajos piped up.

"Why do your people take everything from us?" He was staring at me. His friends joined in with magnificent war whoops.

"Your people killed our ancestors, stole our land, and now keep us out here. There is nothing out here! Nothing!" His voice was high-pitched, nasal, and shrill. "You kill our fathers, you take our sisters, and you turn our brothers into this!" He pointed at Atene.

"He did nothing to you!" Atene shouted.

Unable to contain his anger any longer, the young man jumped to his feet and threw the nearly empty bottle of fortified wine against the back wall of the building. Boom! Glass and wine rained down over us.

"You think you can assimilate us—but you can't!" He reached down and grasped a piece of broken glass. "We do not want you here. No one gave you permission to come onto our land!"

Atene stood, "He is with me!"

Realizing the situation was going to get ugly, I got to my feet.

"You have taken everything from us, but you cannot take my life—only I can do that!" He extended his arm and drew the piece of glass down along the soft skin of the inside of his arm. His friends were staggering around, screaming something.

"You can try to save me, but it is no use. I am as good as dead!"

I did not move to save him. The thought had never entered my mind.

He extended his arm out to show us his blood, but surprisingly there was none. His friends took a closer look. An expression of shock came over his face and his friends cried out to the heavens.

"Sit down and shut up!" Atene said.

"We will drink ourselves to death then," the young man said. "We are The People!"

Suddenly, the young man rushed forward toward me, but before I could move to protect myself, Atene—the ex-United States Army Ranger—stood between us and absorbed his tribesman's anger. "Go! Quickly!" Brigham said. "Go, my friend of Nam."

Just as my reverie ended, I looked up to see Brigham's truck pulling into the parking lot. He had spotted me and was smiling. We got out of our vehicles and embraced. His eyes were clear and as black as night. His movements were spry and energetic. Brigham finally made it home. His father and mother were gone and his sisters had taken other lives, but when he returned to this land, he was home. The land of his birth was sacred, and Atene attributed it to making him well again.

Brigham was finally the man he might have been had he not descended into the flames. He had become a teacher and a respected elder. "I took the long way home," he once told me. "I left for Vietnam and didn't know I was on a journey to find my manhood until I arrived back home years later."

From the 7-11 store we drove out onto the reservation to meet an eighty-year-old Navajo medicine man, Nat Tahonnie, who lived on Big Mountain. As a boy, Nat was a friend of Dog Ears Begay, whom Everett knew. Everett wrote that he, Begay, and other young Navajos stayed up all night once, dancing and singing.

When we arrived at Tahonnie's encampment, he and his seventy-five-year-old sister, Alice, were trying to break a piece of metal welded to their water well pump the day before by two Hopi Bureau of Indian Affairs policemen. The weld had rendered the well inoperable, and without water, Tahonnie, Alice, and the rest of the family would be forced to leave their home.

Tahonnie and Alice are refusniks: they refuse to leave a portion of land claimed by both the Hopi and the Navajo tribes but recently held to be the Hopis'. The dispute between the Hopi and Navajo over land preceded the formation of the United States of America; but since the Lincoln administration, the U.S. government has attempted to mediate. The result has been distrust and resentment from both tribes. In 1974, the U.S. Congress passed the Hopi-Navajo Land Settlement Act, partitioning lands used by both tribes. This agreement was supposed to put an end to the dispute over ownership of the land once and for all. Under the act, lands previously designated for joint use between the tribes were divided equally between the two. The Hopi who were living on areas designated to be Navajo moved off the land. Most of the Navajo moved from lands deemed to be Hopi, but a few, those living on the sacred Big Mountain, refused relocation and now were being threatened with forceful eviction.

Tahonnie was happy to see Brigham, and they embraced warmly. They spoke in Navajo for a long time while I stood around unacknowledged. The Navajo are a formal people, and the protocol for meeting someone requires patience. After a while, Brigham mentioned my name and then Everett's. Tahonnie turned my way without looking at me, nodded his head, and walked away.

"He will sit in council with us," Brigham said, "but he needs to change his shirt first."

When Tahonnie reappeared he was wearing a blue satin shirt and white headband. He led us to his ceremonial hogan, and inside he graciously pointed to the places he wanted us to sit. Alice was already in the hogan but ignored our entrance as though we were not there. Tahonnie sat Indian style on a piece of carpet and began telling us of an ancient Navajo legend about the apocalypse. Brigham served as interpreter.

"If we are moved from this place, Mother Earth will react," Tahonnie said. "We on Big Mountain are being protected by the Great Spirit. We are all under the direction of the Great Spirit. That is the way the story has been handed down from the start of time."

I examined the ceremonial hogan. It was clean and unadorned, the only thing hanging on the walls was a bunch of dried plants wrapped with string. At the center of the structure sat a stove made from an old twenty-gallon metal container. It had been fitted with a small hinged door on the front and a stovepipe on top that protruded out the roof.

Alice sat across from me. She was the most beautiful Navajo I had ever seen. Her skin was golden and she possessed classic cheekbones and full lips. The two most extraordinary things about Alice's beauty were her thick shock of white hair and her dramatically expressive wrinkled face. As Alice listened to her brother's story, her wrinkles pooled languidly around her eyes and mouth. When Nat's voice rose up to make a point, Alice's wrinkles came alive, rising up on her forehead and creating rainbow-like arcs and happy crow's feet at the temples. Alice's wrinkles were aural; they spoke of the spirit and soul within. She was a queen.

Alice was kneeling, sitting on her legs. She wore a scarlet-colored velvet dress. She combed through her hair slowly and rubbed lotion into her hands and elbows. She did not acknowledge us, and we tried not to acknowledge her. For the Navajo, it is impolite to look at a person when first meeting her. Try as I might, I could not take my eyes from her.

As Tahonnie spoke in a lyrical, singsongy cadence, a beautiful young girl about sixteen years old entered and attended to Alice's needs. The girl sat at attention facing Alice and handing her cosmetics. The girl's attentiveness was not that of a dutiful child or devoted servant, but it was that special attentiveness reserved for an honored elder.

Tahonnie was on a roll. When he finished the story of the apocalypse, he eagerly explained about what happened to his water well.

"The welding of the well head is not the first thing they have done to us," he said sitting with one leg folded neatly underneath him, his torso swaying back and forth. "First, they came and bulldozed our grazing land. 'What will we feed our sheep and goats,' we asked? When we moved our stock, they came with a truck and impounded our animals." Tears welled up in Tahonnie's eyes. "'What will we fed the babies?' we asked."

Alice fidgeted. She had been patient long enough. Her brother could not or would not say what else happened yesterday when the BIA policemen sealed the water well. She would do it for him. "My brother won't tell you this," she said. "My brother is a strong warrior and a proud man. . . . When the BIA showed up yesterday, he tried to stop them, and they beat him up!"

Alice's movements were delicate and her face serene. She gazed placidly into some inner or outer world; I could not tell which. She pulled a brush slowly through her thick white hair, pausing to straighten her posture. Suddenly, her shoulders fell and she broke down. Her face was instantly transformed into pools, circles, and potholes.

"The BIA beats up old men," she said. "No one can stop them. They want us to leave our homes, but we will never go."

She lowered her head and spoke to the earthen floor, "We are very old and frightened. This is our home—the only home we have ever known. We have lived on this land since the time of the Creator."

In my peripheral vision, I could see Brigham and Tahonnie sitting at attention, as if a strong current of electricity were rushing through them.

Alice pointed out through the doorway. "We collect herbs out there; our ancestors are buried there. We cannot leave." In an elegant and soft defiance, she concluded, "The Creator is the only one who will relocate me!"

Later that evening, Tahonnie, Brigham, and I walked out across the barren rock and windswept land. Big Mountain is not a mountain at all; while the land rises up to the north slightly, there is no mountain.

"Long before the Anglo arrived," Tahonnie said, "the land was just the land. No one owned it. The Creator made it for all the people—the Dineh, the Hopi, and anyone who came this way. We did not need papers of ownership or fences or the forces of policemen. We would meet the Hopi on the roadway and trade mutton for corn. There was no dispute between we two peoples."

Tahonnie continued his story as we entered a chaparral filled with chest-high sagebrush, then fell silent for a long time. He led us in and out of the sagebrush until we were deep within the colony.

Tahonnie turned to me, "Why are you trailing a man who is dead?"

"He is of great interest to me," I said.

"He is dead!"

"Everett's journey is important to my people."

"He is dead. It will do you no good to try to find him. He is gone. Leave him alone."

Tahonnie stood on the opposite side of a tall aqua-tipped sagebrush as we talked. Cascading clumps of cobalt-colored sage berries surrounded his angelic face. A breeze made the clumps appear to cascade around him like water rushing around a granite boulder.

"I want to see the world as Everett saw it."

"Why?" he asked, lowering his eyes.

"My people have lost part of ourselves. There might be a chance that by following in Everett's footprints I can trace a path back to what we have lost."

Tahonnie stared at me—or into me—for a long time. The sage berries caught the sunset, and Tahonnie's face floated on the shimmering watery surface.

Turning to Brigham, Tahonnie spoke in Dineh again: "I remember long ago when from over there," he pointed to a nearby ridge with his head and lips, "we bedded the sheep down for the night, and the young man, known to us as Everett, entered our camp. We did not know him and we were all very afraid. He gave us no warning. Imagine, a white man entering an Indian camp! This is not something that happens.

"When he arrived, we were singing songs and he suddenly appeared across the fire from us. We stopped singing. We looked at him and at one another. We thought he was crazy. He did not speak to us, only smiled and nodded his head. He talked to his dog and his two horses. After a while, he sat down next to the fire. He pulled tobacco from his pouch and rolled cigarettes. He began to sing Anglo songs that we did not know. It was very funny, and he smiled at us."

Tahonnie smiled widely and his white teeth contrasted with the sage. Turning to me, he said, "The man you follow was crazy. Maybe you are right to follow his trail."

Tahonnie wagged a finger at me. "But my advice to you, Anglo, is that it is never a good idea to follow a dead man. Bad medicine! You can end up dead yourself."

"Will you take me to your camp, the place where Everett surprised you?" I asked.

Without waiting for Brigham to translate, Tahonnie turned and headed toward the ridge and the campsite. He stopped at an old fire ring, nodded his head, and pointed with his lips.

For some reason, every time I stand where Everett stood, I feel zapped by some inexplicable power. We three stood there silently for a long time.

When we arrived back in camp, it was long after dark, and the beautiful young Navajo girl who attended to Alice was waiting for us. She motioned for me to follow her, never letting her eyes meet mine. She took me to Alice's one-room wooden house next to the ceremonial hogan. The house was lit by candles and kerosene lamps. Magnificent Navajo rugs covered the floor, hung from the walls, and were draped across her bed.

Alice invited me to sit in a straight wooden chair. She spoke excellent English. She sat on a rug-covered couch.

"You are looking for the young white boy, Everett?"

I nodded my head, trying not to look directly at her.

"It is so long ago," Alice said softly. "I have not heard his name or thought of his face in many years. But, I still remember it well."

I could not believe what I was hearing.

"I was fourteen and my big brother, Nat, brought Everett to our camp. He took his hat off when we were introduced. He only stayed three days, helping with a sheep corral, but no one forgot him. When we learned he had disappeared, we were all very sad. He was so young and beautiful."

A shiver raced up my spine. Something very important was happening. I sat quietly, listening.

"You are writing a book about him?"

"Yes."

"I have never told anyone this," Alice admitted, "but I will tell you so you can write about it."

"Thank you."

"The night before Everett left us, we walked together under the stars. It is not right for a young Dineh girl to be alone with an Anglo after dark, but I could not help myself. I will never forget the stars and the breeze and the fragrances that night." Alice lowered her head and fell silent for a long time.

"The next morning, Everett packed his horses and rode away. We all told him to come back." Alice was reliving her experience, and I somehow felt I was part of it—as though I were there.

Alice smiled, she had remembered something else. "Sitting atop his horse, just as he was leaving, he turned to me and told me I was the most beautiful girl he had ever seen. My whole family was standing there, and I was so embarrassed that all I could do was hang my head and blush." Alice blushed again, nearly sixty years later. "I was just a young girl then, and I could not stop myself. That was the last time I ever saw him. Once, years later, I thought I heard him calling me, but when I turned in the direction of his voice, it was only the wind."

CHAPTER FIVE

BRIGHAM ATENE

A few days later Brigham and I drove out across the reservation over endless dirt roads that embroidered the land like some intricately woven fabric. We stopped at the shacks and hogans of elders who might have known Everett. We went from place to place all day long, but no one could help us. In the late afternoon as we passed a line of hogans with giant piles of garbage and wrecked automobiles stacked next to them, I asked Brigham a question, "If your people love the sacred Mother Earth, why do so many pile trash next to their houses?"

Atene turned to look at me and smiled widely. "We do love Mother Earth, but when we discard something because its usefulness is gone, we do not see it anymore. In a way, it no longer exists for us."

"That's easy for you to say," I said.

"You have a point, my friend," Atene said. He spoke in the beautiful tone of Dineh elders, the voice that is so easy to love. "The cars and junk and garbage do exist, but we do not see them. It is the Navajo way. You Anglo do the same thing. There is much in your world that you do not see."

"Like what?"

"For one, you do not see your homeless people living in the streets. You do not see them because in your hearts you are homeless, too. I know this is true; I lived among you. For you, these images and dolmen, these lost people of the streets, remind you of your own homelessness, so you refuse to acknowledge them."

I protested. "We have homes!"

"Your soul has no home, Anglo. It has no home because you do not honor it. You do not honor it or the Creator or our Mother Earth. You only honor your own ingenuity and money. You destroy the earth and you are blinded to all that connects you to your grief, pain, and past."

Atene had a point, so I quickly conceded, hoping he would spare me the details.

Later, as we drove into an ever-receding eastern horizon, I thought about what Atene had said. Many people of my generation are lost and are making a long and painful odyssey that delivers them to despair, defeat, and near-death before they ascend to stand tall once again like Brigham Atene. This odyssey takes a decade or more, and when it is finished, they arrive home once again. These people are tempered and strengthened by the fire of mistakes and defeats they have survived. Only then are they ready to take their rightful places as leaders and sources of wisdom.

I remembered what Brigham had said about taking the long way home. "I didn't know I was on a journey to find my manhood until I arrived back home years later." This made sense to me. In New Guinea, the aboriginal Donne tribe believes that before a boy's ascent into manhood can begin, he must first descend into the flames and be covered with ashes. Every facet of the boy's descent into the flames and his ascent into manhood is overseen by the elders and is celebrated by the entire tribe.

By contrast, the journey from boyhood to manhood for American boys is taken alone. The descent into the flames begins much earlier; most boys are raised without fathers or the participation of older men. Without any knowledge or helpful examples of what it means to be a man, American boys are sent out into the world to find their own way by trial and error. This pathway takes years to negotiate and is marked by confusion, mistake, heartache, and defeat.

MONUMENT VALLEY

Early the next morning I packed my car and drove to the north end of Monument Valley. On a little-used dirt road, hidden from the highway by a hill, I parked and hiked off into the puzzle of ridges and valleys and flat-top plateaus toward El Capitan, a famous monolith in the valley. From the roadway, El Capitan looked to be several hours away, but as I hiked toward it, it seemed to back off, moving farther away from me. The ground was carved by erosion and warped by pressure, taking me on side trips through intricate mazes of glens, grottoes, fissures, and passageways. I let my feet carry me, honoring the path as it presented itself, taking shapes and directions and detours I could not have predicted.

As I stopped to eat some raisins and have a cool drink of water, I noticed some mysterious shadowy canyons to the east. I decided not to capture their magic by exploring them. I have long resented science for its many revelations; when science solves a problem, the magic surrounding it evaporates. We unravel the secrets of the natural world, too, reducing them to basic scientific principles, and in doing so, we devalue them. We do the same thing to our spirit and soul as well. Instead of honoring the magic of our inner workings as it presents itself, we attempt to pick it apart as a scientist might, and something gets lost along the way.

I continued on, catching glimpses of El Capitan occasionally as I crested a hill or skirted around a bronze- or vermilion-colored canyon system. It was much farther than I thought, and in the middle of the silence and burning rock, I felt the weight of my optimism surrendering to the shadow of doubt and self-criticism that defeated me as a younger man. My nostrils filled with the ripe, pungent perfume of sagebrush, while unnamed shades of umber, violet, and blue surrounded me as I made my way down into a canyon.

One footfall at a time, I went down into the labyrinth of my past defeats. The sun was on my face, and the shadows were all around me. Down I went into the place of dead ends, twisting canyons of excruciating pain and foolish self-centered narcissism. Down where the textures of the land are paradox: dried mud flats and countersunk potholes, overhangs and interlocking sediments, siltstone and stone sand dunes. The multiplicity of this nature—of my nature—demanded that I make this descent as part of my odyssey.

I slipped by degrees into the lunacy that so characterizes modern man. I saw the images of the sons I sired but did not father. They stood defiantly before me on pillars of broken sandstone. The friends and lovers I retreated from are there too, crouching next to the alligator junipers. "I am guilty," I said out loud. The lies I told back then—I knew so little about life and even less about myself. I did not intend to hurt anyone, but everywhere I turned I created pain. The more I learned about myself, the more important it became to get away. The ancient, ancient lies and the profoundly troubling mistakes of my youth—one by one, they wafted down to me from the hot wings of Artemis, the Goddess of Solitude.

The aboriginal Donne flutes called out to the boy in me. Descend into the ashes, they sang, before rising into the light of manhood. But, it is more difficult in my culture, I said. The descent takes much longer. I am the only person who can grant me forgiveness, and I have learned I must refuse. Like the Greek god Prometheus, lashed to a rock and destined to have his liver ripped from his abdomen every new day, I must stand tall, bare my chest, and wait with arms outstretched. I promised I would always remember the hurt and pain I have caused. I am truly sorry.

I walked on through the tears until I could see as a child sees, and the wonder and magic of my own mysterious life returned. I understood the voices of lunacy and the need to face my demons. For me, peace lies along the simple dirt path before me. From it, I can view my life stretching out before me and behind me. The path affords me a fresh vision and the necessary idealism to face the world at large. My modern culture wants me to side-step negative moods and emotions, yet the simple path into wilderness forces me to observe what is really within my heart and soul. Nature befriends my problems, it allows for my mistakes, and it offers me the latitude to be human.

It is not enough to seek only the light. To find true peace, I must visit the land of shadow and defeat. I must walk along the hot and dusty path to the place where my shadow resides. The true spirit of transcendence and the lofty quest for the highest vision are found along this trail.

Picking my way out of the canyon, I spotted El Capitan on the southern horizon. I was no closer to it than when I began. From some high turrets I watched the heat shimmering off the burning hogback ridges between me and the obelisk. This place possessed the special beauty of all wild and lonely things. At the horizon, spread out across its length, sail-like clouds touched the alabaster towers of the valley. I remembered what Everett wrote to his friend Bill about Monument Valley:

> It has all been a beautiful dream, sometimes tranquil, some-times fantastic, and with enough pain and tragedy to make the delights possible by contrast. But the pain too has been unreal. The whole dream has been filled with warm and cool but per-fect colors and aesthetic contemplations. . . . Alone on the open desert I have made up songs of wild, poignant rejoicing and transcendent melancholy.

I would not make it to El Capitan that day. Perhaps I will never make it that far. After a long rest, I turned back, descending into the shadowy canyon behind me, not making it back to my car until long after dark.

It was probably difficult for people in the 1930s to fathom what a young person such as Everett would be doing out in the hostile wilderness. Modern conveniences such as refrigerators, air conditioners, electric stoves, radios, record players, and films were drawing Americans indoors rather than out-doors. At the same time, the Great Depression was causing hardship enough; why would someone bring more on himself?

While Everett's parents were supportive of his travels, even encouraging him at first, his father, Christopher, was concerned about Everett's education and future. In letters written from 1930 to 1933, Everett sold the merits of his vagabond life to almost everyone, especially his father.

Everett's travels and adventures made for great reading, and his letters were filled with beautiful descriptions of the land and thoughtful analysis of what the grand spectacle of nature was doing to him. The natural world made Everett come alive, and his letters expressed this superbly. Remarkably, the images he created of the land captured both the tremendous life force of nature as well as its ability to heal, soothe, and invigorate. On this land, he was alive in ways few people know. Today, these written images are his greatest gift to us.

By 1934, whether Everett knew it or not, he was offering arguments and evidence in his letters that his wandering was not just a lark; the vagabond life and the search for beauty might well be the direction his life was meant to follow. His original motive for striking out had much more to do with romance and adventure than with finding a deeper sense of himself.

When Everett arrived in Monument Valley for the first time in 1931, he decided to take a brush name, Lan Rameau. To his family, he implored: "Please respect my brush name. It is hard to lead a dual existence. The first name begins with L not S. How do you say it in French, *Nomme de Boushe*, or what?"

Eventually, Everett dropped his brush name, but before he did he wrote to his friend Bill about it: "As to my pen name, although it is really a brush name, I am still in turmoil, but I think that I will heroically stand firm in the face of all misunderstanding and mispronunciations. I'll simply lead a dual existence."

Everett was a teenager, one moment sophisticated and the next naive and goofy. It is easy to see why this brash and adventurous youth was so attractive and easy to like. It is also easy to see why his parents worried about him. Personal growth is never easy nor is it easy to watch. Everett was endearing and painfully vulnerable. The Navajo and their secretive Hopi neighbors viewed him with awe, referring to him as the "crazy but wonderful white boy," according to Nat Tahonnie.

Out in the desert, Everett's pocketbook contained only his good nature and the strength to see the real value of his voyage. He walked hundreds of miles to work for food or to save a few pennies, sketching and making block prints—selling them to whomever he could find and for whatever he could get. He went without. In a letter to Bill, he answered the question of how he existed:

> How do I subsist? That's a good question. I often wonder myself. However, when I'm broke, something always turns up. . . . Recently, I sold a sketch to a clerk in a lumber camp for $5. One print brought a dollar. Now when my total monetary wealth is four cents, a letter informs me that a print of my mother's, which she copied from a painting of mine, brought a $25 prize and I am to have $10 of it in the course of time . . .

When Everett wasn't struggling against hunger or his family's concern or society's condemnation for his lack of conformity, he was comparing himself to his friends and the lives they were living. He was strident in his assessments, often asking them how they managed to endure their meaningless lives in the city while juxtaposing the beautiful and rewarding life he led in the wild.

At the same time, Everett was chastising his older brother, Waldo, for the choices of his life. Theirs was the special, turbulent relationship of brothers who love one another deeply yet who find an imperative in carping. Since we do not have Waldo's letters to Everett, this brotherhood can be glimpsed only in Everett's correspondence to him. In a 1931 letter, Everett quips,

> . . . But you are probably enjoying life anyhow, even though you do not live it to the fullest . . . I, myself, would sooner walk a whole day behind the burro than spend two hours on the streetcar. What are your plans for the future? Are you preparing yourself for a better job, are you ignorant of your own desires, or are you leaving your life to circumstance?
>
> Somehow, I am very glad not to be home, where civilized life thrusts the thought of money upon one from all sides. With an adequate stock of provisions, I can forget the cursed stuff, or blessed stuff, for days and weeks at a time.
>
> Your censure was quite deserved in regard to providing my needs, but remember that I have asked for no money and that of the equipment I asked for was unprocurable here, and necessary to my life.

After two years of wandering through the warm months and spending winters at the family home in Los Angeles, at the behest of his father, Everett entered UCLA. It was the fall of 1932, and presidential candidates Franklin Roosevelt and Herbert Hoover made whistle-stops across the country. From his red, white, and blue flag-festooned caboose, Roosevelt outlined his ideas for change, later to be known as the New Deal. In Germany, Hitler's Socialist party swept into power on the whispering winds of economic disaster.

At UCLA, Everett studied, yet he was dissatisfied, unhappy, and felt out of place. After just one quarter, he dropped out of school and waited for the weather to break so he could return to the wilderness. To a friend, he explained that the university was a valuable episode, but he did not let it get a stranglehold on him. To another friend, Bob, Everett was cavalier: "How little you know me to think that I could still be in the university. How could a lofty, unconquerable soul like mine remain imprisoned in that academic backwater, wherein all but the most docile wallow in a hopeless slough . . . "

Everett's decision to leave UCLA troubled his father. It is not known how Christopher broached this subject with his son, but in the next letter segment, Everett vigorously defended his decision to drop out of college. He also staked out new territory in his relationship with his father. Undoubtedly, Everett loved, respected,55

and admired his father, yet he was becoming more confident about who he really was. From his San Francisco boardinghouse in 1933, Everett wrote:

> For myself, I am doing my best to have variety and intensity of experience, and largely succeeding, I think. I see no grounds for complaint on that score. There is no need for fearing that I will be a "one-sided" freak artist, to use your phrase, for I am interested almost equally in all the arts and in human relations and reactions as well.
>
> As to this half-baked pother about my always feeling inferior in the presence of college graduates, that fear is groundless too. I am not nonplused in the presence of anybody, and I am seldom at a loss with anyone I am interested in.
>
> As to the million-dollar endowment of going through the college mill, I have a three million dollar endowment already, that I am sure of, and I don't have to go begging. I have my very deep sensitivities to beauty, to music and to nature. In addition, thanks to you and mother, I have an intellect that is capable of analysis and of grappling with things almost anywhere I turn.
>
> I am learning things all the time, and I certainly have never felt any handicap with Fiske and Schermerhorn [relatives Everett visited while in San Francisco]. I could not do the things they are doing, but on the other hand, they are shoved into such a rut by their work that they cannot follow any of the broadly cultural lines that I follow, and I certainly do not regret my freedom. On all sides I meet people who are not able to follow things up as I am doing, and it is not I who envy them.
>
> You can be ashamed of me if you like, but you cannot make me feel ashamed of myself, in that direction at least. Waldo has an entirely different problem and I don't think it is profitable to compare us as you do.
>
> As for me, I have tasted your cake and I prefer your unbuttered bread. I don't wish to withdraw from life to college, and I have a notion, conceited or not, that I know what I want from life, and can act upon it.

Years after Everett's disappearance, his father better understood his son's special nature. In his diary Christopher wrote, "The older person does not realize the soul-flights of the adolescent. I think we all poorly understood Everett."

I suspect Christopher Ruess understood Everett quite well. He was a man of philosophy and religious inquiry. While Christopher's diary entry shows his caring and sensitivity, it also carries another, opposite, and contradictory message about how his generation devalued the highly personal search for one's true self.

Soul-flights are only partially understood, and the true value of personal inquiry is minimized. Perhaps the most important thing to know about soul-flights, or quests for personal enlightenment, is that they are not just the property of adolescence. The quest belongs to us all; it begins at birth and continues throughout life.

By July 1934, Everett was experiencing the benefits of his quiet meander. His letters exhibit tremendous growth and a greater understanding of his real nature. Everett was riding the cutting edge of life. In his book *Lila*, author and philosopher Robert Pirsig calls it dynamic quality, the pre-intellectual understanding on some level about what is right for you; or, a predisposition to pursue a course of action toward quality without conscious knowledge or even effort on your part. This dynamic quality is the magic surrounding all that we do.

To Bill, Everett wrote:

> *Once more I am roaring drunk with the lust of life and adventure and unbearable beauty. I have the devil's own conception of a perfect time; adventure seems to beset me on all quarters without my even searching for it; I find gay comradeships and lead the wild, free life wherever I am. And yet, there is always an undercurrent of restlessness and a wild longing. . . . I shall always be a rover.*
>
> *Alone I shoulder the sky and hurl my defiance and shout the song of the conqueror to the four winds, earth, sea, sun, moon, and stars. I LIVE!*

Moreover, Everett's original reason for making the quest was forgotten along the way; the internal and external currents carried him from one new place to another as well as from the outside to the inside until he was changed. In a real sense, Everett had arrived at a place where just a few years earlier he could not have fully appreciated. His original intent was to use his experiences in nature to fuel his art and poetry, yet by July 1934, just a few short months before his disappearance, the true inquisitor and lover of life had emerged and was growing into a fuller person.

JOHN UPTON TERRELL

The best investigation into Everett's disappearance was conducted by the

Salt Lake Tribune and its ace reporter, John Upton Terrell, in July 1935. At the behest of the mysterious Captain Neal Johnson and eight months after the last-known sighting of Everett, the *Tribune* dispatched Terrell south from Salt Lake into the unexplored and untamed wild country of southern Utah and northern Arizona.

In the 1930s no telephone lines existed south of Blanding, Utah, nor were there any real roadways. For two weeks, Terrell and Johnson struggled over rutted, horse-drawn wagon trails in a Model-T Ford, picking paths over dangerous slickrock formations, fording rivers and sandy washes to finally reach far into Indian country where they visited the nomadic camps of the Navajo.

Captain Neal Johnson did not know Everett and was drawn into the search for reasons of his own. According to locals in Escalante and southern Utah, Johnson was considered a shady character. It was said that Johnson told people he was raised in Hanksville, Utah, but no one there could substantiate this claim. He also told people he had been a captain in the Mexican Air Force and had seen action in the Mexican Civil War.

Shortly after Everett's disappearance was discovered, Johnson appeared at the Ruess family home in Los Angeles and offered his assistance. Johnson knew the country and was confident he could discover Everett's whereabouts, but he needed money to capitalize his search. Over the next fourteen months, Johnson was to bring hope, frustration, despair, and resignation to the Ruess family.

In John Terrell's four-part series, which the *Tribune* published upon his return in August, he wove a fascinating tale of Everett's disappearance. Terrell's account began at a midnight council with a trance-induced medicine man and his psychic wife; it ended three weeks later when he, Captain Johnson, and famed Navajo tracker Dougi returned from a dangerous journey taking them north from Navajo Mountain to Everett's last-known campsite in Davis Gulch.

When Terrell and Captain Johnson arrived in Kayenta, they were instructed to visit the respected medicine man Natani at his remote camp far out in the wild. If anyone knew where Everett was or what might have happened to him, it would be Natani. Terrell, Johnson, and their interpreter arrived at Natani's camp long after dark. After a few confusing minutes of introductions and explanations, Natani nodded his head and surprised them by saying he had been expecting them. Published August 27, 1935, the story of this meeting is described by Terrell:

> *Natani had opened his shirt and drawn out a medicine bag.*
> *His wife had covered her face. Almost at the moment he began*

to chant softly the rain fell. *Great large drops spattered on the sand and sagebrush. We sat huddled over, but in a few minutes our backs were soaked. There was no stopping now. No one moved. The chant grew louder, but never rising above the singsong rhythmic way the Navajo medicine man calls upon his gods. Natani's wife weaved slowly back and forth. She lifted her shoulders. Dipping into the sacred little buckskin bag, Natani drew out a pinch of medicine dust and sprinkled it over his wife, not for an instant hesitating in his "singing."*

She suddenly uncovered her face, bent forward and let her finger run through the sand. Twice she threw the "earth" over her bosom. In the sand she built a mound; she indicated crooked lines running from it. I knew then that she was building Navajo Mountain, the sacred mountain that rises up 150 miles north and west of Kayenta and I tried to recall what I had heard about this Indian shrine. On its timbered top certain gods come down to the earth. It is hallowed ground, no place for mortal Indian, and no Navajo ever remains on it after sundown. All day he may hunt horses on its great rough slopes, or hunt [other game], but always he starts down as the sun falls. At darkness the mountain is left to the gods.

Natani's wife twice destroyed the miniature mountain her quick hands built. It was not right, or perhaps she had erred in following her spiritual instructions. Patiently she built it a third time, never raising her eyes to look on other faces. Natani sang, moving his thin shoulders slightly with the rhythm of his song, his voice fine and resonant, beauty in every tone. The rain grew colder, fell harder.

Now the mountain was finished, the crooked lines running from it [the deep canyons] apparently were drawn satisfactorily. To the north of the mountain Natani's wife drew a long line twisting and running generally southward. From this line a finger trailed almost directly east, leaving a smaller, though no less twisted, line. The converging point of these two lines was almost directly north of the sacred mountain, perhaps in the scale of her map a distance of 30 miles. They were the Colorado and San Juan Rivers.

The chanting ended abruptly. Natani's wife sat with head fallen, breathing deeply, as if she were very tired. The rain stopped, the cloud bank breaking and drifting across the brilliant starry sky in small fragments.

"Go to the forks of the rivers," Natani spoke.

"He [Everett] lives there?" my guide asked.

"He was there. Close by he made a camp. You will find the fire."

"Have you seen him [in a vision]?" the guide inquired.

"He has gone away from there."

"He is dead?"

"He has gone away and does not mean to come back."

"He went away without his camp outfit?"

"I do not see that clearly. There is a shadow. Only some of his outfit was moved away. There is more some places, I see him talking with two friends. They are Navajos. Young men like himself. They sing and eat together. Then there is a shadow. He has gone away. The Navajos have left the place. They are no longer with him. She [his wife] says they have traveled together. He [Ruess] has given himself to our gods. He has taken us in his arms and wished to come among us."

"Does she say he came into the Navajo country?"

"She says he did not. He went away there where he camped."

During the next two days we talked with white traders, with government men of long experience among the Indians, with white guides and stockmen who not only speak the Navajo tongue, but understand the Indian customs and characters. Invariably, upon hearing Natani's message, they gave one answer: "Do as he told you."

"You can take it lightly if you want to," one old trader said, "and I wouldn't believe in Indian medicine either. But I learned long ago never to laugh at it. I've seen too many strange things happen. Those fellows are uncanny, and if I were you I'd head straight for the forks of the river."

Terrell wrote that, in all likelihood, what Natani had said was a combination of information he had already learned about Everett as well as psychic prophesy.

CHAPTER SIX

NAVAJO MOUNTAIN

From the dusty, garbage-lined dirt road leading to Navajo Mountain, I watched Monument Valley recede in my rearview mirror, and as I did, I started the process of planning my return. This valley always enjoins me in a conversation that is never complete, one that invariably ends with the need for further discussion.

The solitary monuments of the valley invited me to observe my own capacity for darkness and shadow. Somehow, these lofty towers stand in contrast to the deep tributaries of my soul. Aspirations are so high and mighty here, I cannot help but feel insignificant and small. I am also invited to think about my time on earth here. While the open deserts and mesa country cleanse my palate, bringing the sweet taste of new eternities, the stalwart obelisks of this valley empower the corrosive bile of my decay.

I will be gone soon, and nothing of me will remain. The sun will rise, and the sun will set, and the valley of monuments will remain as it is. While my culture insists I look only at the bright side—at the cost of clarity and truth—Monument Valley allows me to consider my own darkness and the frailty of all life.

When Everett left Kayenta, he and his two burros bushwhacked 100 miles west where they climbed the heaping shoals of Navajo Mountain. I followed along behind him—only a moment later by the geologic clock—spending a night in a secret cottonwood oasis.

Cottonwood puffs floated among seeds of timothy and fescue on a cushion of heavy viscous air at the oasis. Unnamed fragrances of erotic earth floated lithely around me, coming from both near and far. Songbirds and finches darted from tree to bush, singing the songs of mating, while blue-black ravens carved voluptuous figure eights around the great cottonwood tops.

At the edge of a seasonal creek, thickets of red river birch gently undulated to the evening breeze. The birch's shiny shafts caught the last rays of sunlight and reflected an eerie twilight to me. I did not fully occupy my life in this place. I was all parts and pieces floating upward into the twilight and downward onto the earth.

The images of nature were so beautiful, so perfect, so utterly unbelievable that somehow they forced a doorway into my interior to crack open. Behind this doorway the world of possibility I knew as a child existed. It is the place where everything makes "magical sense," and this magic is woven into the core of my being. Nature asks little of me except to be who I am and to show the magic of my own special nature. The truth of what this magic can do is a deeply personal thing.

Over the years I have learned to come to this land alone. These solitary pilgrimages help me to acknowledge the feelings I own. The experiences of wandering, longing, separation, adventure, silence, and solitude somehow help me in this process of knowing myself. These experiences feed and enrich me, serving to focus a sharper sense of my own uniqueness.

Within this lusty grove of cottonwoods, I felt at peace about my dear friend Nancy's terminal cancer. I've known Nancy longer than any of my other female friends and, despite the pain of her impending demise, the mysterious web of solace encompassed me there.

"It is all right, my friend," Nancy spoke to me from the round table within. "I will live on, Mark. One day soon we will be together again."

"Nancy," I said, "you can't sit at the table. You're not even dead yet!"

Nancy fell silent.

An image of Nancy appeared before me; it came from the archaeological file of my memory. I held the image still and fine-focused it, but it quickly faded into the sepia tones of aged photographs. The image was a collage of the first time Nancy and I met. We were sitting in a 1957 Chevy at the Ute Drive-In Theatre. It was the summer of 1965, and Elvis Presley danced and sang "Vee-vaaa Las Vegas" across the wide screen. I refocused the image again and for a time it was perfect, but then it yellowed and completely faded away. The image was gone. The 1957 Chevy was gone. The Ute Drive-In was gone—turned into an upscale apartment complex. Elvis was gone. And soon, Nancy, too, would be gone.

The author Thomas Moore said that when we reflect on the tragedies of our own lives, when we slowly find our way through their miseries, we are being initiated into the mysterious ways of the soul. This makes good sense, and for me nature is the means of entry into the mysterious ways of my soul. Nature keeps me on the labyrinthine path. If I can honor the path as it presents itself, taking shapes and directions I would never have predicted or desired, then I am on the way to discovering the lower levels of inner peace. The deep value of life reveals itself slowly and paradoxically along the way.

The first of my friends to pull a chair up to the round table of my inner dialogues was Sylvia Knight. Sylvia was just thirteen years old, and I was seventeen when we met at Murray Park in my hometown during a Fourth of July fireworks celebration. Sylvia was already tall, willowy, blonde, and very beautiful. Sylvia and I were in love. It was a secret unspoken love, yet we both knew it. If Sylvia would have lived, we would still be together.

Just four years later, the same week she was crowned homecoming queen at Murray High School, Sylvia was dead. It happened on a warm and lovely April evening in 1971 as she drove to my place for dinner. A drunk driver ran a red light and BAM! It was all over in an instant; her life was snuffed out.

Sylvia's arrival at the round table came a few months later as I raced my motorcycle up nearby Big Cottonwood Canyon, adjacent to Salt Lake City. The truth is I had planned to join her that day and was accelerating around a sharp corner, traveling as fast as my motorcycle would go. Centrifugal force carried me to the edge of the road where a 200-foot-deep canyon awaited my arrival. The thread of my life was about to pass through the eyelet of death when time mysteriously slowed down, allowing me to see every tree, rock, and bush far below in the canyon. I was at peace.

Suddenly, Sylvia's voice whispered in my ear. "I am still with you, Mark. I'm really not very far away. I have not left you." Just as suddenly, I was back on the roadway again.

Since Sylvia's death, I have taken care of her grave, spending countless hours trimming the grass around her granite headstone. I have given her bouquets of colorful spring flowers and baskets of autumn leaves. I have made snowmen to share the winter's frozen passage with her. I have seen magnificent sunrises over the Wasatch Mountains east of the city and have gazed up at wistful crescent moons as they dip up the night over the Oquirrh Mountains to the west.

I heard Sylvia's laughter at the oasis that night. She was still a giggly teenager, and I was a serious middle-aged man. She said that I was a fool, but her sanction did not offend me; it warmed me.

The next person to arrive at the round table was my best friend and confidante, Randall Potts. Randall and I were inseparable from the eighth grade to college. We shared all the exciting adventures of the 1960s together: the Beatles; Cassius Clay; JFK's dream, and the nightmare of his assassination; girls; Apollo and man on the moon; the draft and Vietnam. I can't remember a single time when Randall was not at my side.

Somewhere along the way, Randall and I drifted apart. He headed east into the glow of Transcendental Meditation; I headed downward, falling head over heels into my own personal inferno. In retrospect, I realize that Randall Potts could have been the most extraordinary person I had ever known. If there is such a thing as reincarnation—the transcending from this life to an afterlife or to another life—then Randall Potts made the journey.

In 1969 Randall became interested in meditation. Soon after, he moved to Spain and studied with the maharishi. Randall sat at the master's feet. Upon returning to the United States, he taught meditation in the prison systems; he even taught Jimi Hendrix meditation while the rock idol dried out from a drug binge. By 1974, Randall had returned to Salt Lake City where he became the director of a meditation center.

Just days before his death in 1977, Randall and I ran into each other in Sugarhouse at the Pinecone Restaurant. The timeless rapport of old friends is one of life's greatest gifts, and it was marvelous to see him. I had just returned from northern Minnesota where I lived on a dairy farm with devotees of the Rosicrucian Fellowship, and I hadn't seen Randall in nearly a year.

"I know it's going to sound strange," he said, after we bumped into one another, "but I knew you were going to be here this morning."

At the time, I thought his remark was odd, but I did not ask him about it. Actually, there was no way Randall could have known I'd be at the Pinecone that morning. I didn't know myself until an hour before I was there. I had developed a toothache and had scheduled an emergency appointment with a nearby dentist. After arriving at the dentist's office, I was informed that the dentist had another emergency patient, and I would have a two-hour wait. I decided to get coffee and walked two blocks away to the Pinecone.

I had never seen Randall as excited as he was that day. He told me such a strange story, I've been shaking my head ever since. In essence, he said that he had been meditating for more than eight hours a day and, because of it, he believed he was on the verge of a great discovery. He told me that mankind was at the dawning of a new day of enlightenment, and that this new day would be revealed to us all through music.

What Randall told me next stunned me. He fluttered his beautiful pale blue eyes, ashed his cigarette with his long artistic fingers, looked directly into my eyes, and said, "Mark, I think I'm on the verge of knowing the truth about never-ending life."

As Randall spoke, I wondered if he hadn't gone too far. He had always been introspective and a deep thinker, but what he was telling me was all whacked out. Later that day, I wrote down everything he said, and I still have his words. Before we parted that day, Randall thanked me profusely for being his friend throughout the years. He shared with me a few personal reveries about us and our adventures together. I didn't know it at the time, but Randall was telling me good-bye. I invited him to my new apartment on Tuesday of the next week for dinner. He accepted my offer graciously, but like Sylvia, Randall did not make it to my house.

When Randall's body was found that Tuesday, he was sitting in the lotus position. He had died while meditating. He was twenty-nine years old. The autopsy could find nothing wrong expect that there was no air in his lungs. During our last meeting, Randall told me he was practicing Kundalini meditation, a highly advanced form of meditation in which the participant hyperventilates by breathing in and out vigorously and then exhaling slowly. Randall had exhaled all the air from his lungs and voluntarily transcended his bodily bounds.

Later, Randall came to me often. From the round table he spoke matter-of-factly about death as though it were no big deal. He was happier in death than he had been in life. Randall has not come to the table for years now. I sense he has gone on to another new life. The last time I heard his voice, he told me he was proud that I had risen above my melancholy to become a writer. At the same time, he seemed somehow impatient and disappointed at my progress toward enlightenment.

A few years later, Mick arrived, as did my dog-faced-boy, Bask. There are others who come to the round table occasionally. I do not know who they are; they seem to float in and out at the periphery. I suspect they are the people I once was: the small boy wanting desperately to be seen by his father, the idealistic and wounded young man, the halfhearted husband and father.

It was pitch black at the cottonwood grove. The desert stars illuminated the high heavens.

"Oh, Mark," Nancy said, "what will become of you?"

"Nancy! Please Nanc, don't go! Stay here with me, I need you, my friend. We have seen so much together. You are part of me, part of this landscape. Please, please, stay with me."

"Quit whining!" Mick piped up from his chair at the table.

"Fuck you, Mick! Do you think it's easy to lose nearly everyone you love, everyone you have shared the voyage with?"

Silence. Starlight.

"Hey, Mick," I said, "you have no right to criticize me. You don't know what it's like to have your best friend kill himself. You'll never know the excruciating agony of watching someone you love die slowly of cancer."

"I concede," Mick said. "But please remember, Mark, you are not alone."

Two days later, high on the northeastern slope of Navajo Mountain near

War God Springs, I shed my heavy backpack and made camp in a family circle of rare bristlecone pines. Everett camped somewhere nearby. I arranged my sleeping bag next to the eldest tree, which looked as though it had been dead for hundreds of years. Its sinuous, gray, elongated trunk lounged supine on a bed of checkerboard shale, and its twisting limbs praised the heavens exactly as they did a thousand years ago.

This land is in a perpetual state of becoming—it constantly reminds me to think about the shapes of things to come—and yet, the bristlecone pine's dogged permanence offers another metric for contemplation. While this land is as unexpected as tomorrow, always assuring me that it is perfectly natural to make myself over again, the bristlecone pine reminds me that there is not much difference between the appearance of life and that of death.

After I lunched on raisins, apples, and cheese, I gazed out on this Jacob's ladder I had climbed. The land to the north fell away plateau by plateau, rung by rung, into the jumble of broken rock and canyons of the Escalante Drainage where Everett disappeared. Through some unexplainable conjunction of soul and nature, a suspension of time occurred and the present moment looped into a circle and replayed itself again and again. When I was finally aware of myself again, I was muttering a Latin term, *Lacrimae rerum*, or "Ah, the tears of things [nature]." Within the translation is the implicit idea that life and nature are tinged with sadness.

Everett felt this mixed blessing of sadness, solace, and peace. Within the expanse of the natural world, these mixed blessings come in waves carried by beauty, quiet, and wind. Everett wrote about it to his friend Edward while he camped near here:

> *Strange, sad winds sweep down the canyon, roaring in the firs and the tall pines, swaying their crests. I don't know how you feel about it, Edward, but I can never accept life as a matter of course. Much as I seem to have shaped my own way, following after my own thinking and my own desires, I never cease to wonder at the impossibility that I live. Even when to my senses the world is not incredibly beautiful or fantastic, I am overwhelmed by the appalling strangeness and intricacy of the curiously tangled knot of life . . .*

Under blue sky and starry night, Everett traveled all four directions—north, south, east, west—but he also journeyed into the fifth direction, the perpendicular one that goes from the outside of us to the inside.

I believe much of the interest in Everett Ruess lies in the individual's need for someone to point the way to self-enlightenment. This leader needs to be young and untainted by cynicism or unquestioned about motive. He or she needs to be a product of a less-complicated world because we are not. She or he must not be available to us (and our carnivorous media) because our scrutiny would surely bring a person down. And, most importantly, this person must have a message that is communicated unintentionally yet with the force of profound truth and clarity.

Everett's truly prophetic nature sums it up best in a letter written from War God Springs high on Navajo Mountain. Though decades have passed, the wisdom of this young man stings me today: "I have always been unsatisfied with life as most people live it. Always I want to live more intensely and richly. Why muck and conceal one's true longings and loves, when by speaking of them one might find someone to understand them, and by acting on them one might discover one's self."

WAR GOD SPRINGS

After spending five days exploring War God Springs, I pulled on my backpack and set off westward for Rainbow Bridge. I enjoyed my time at the springs. It is easy to see why Everett and many generations of Dineh have journeyed from the low, sweltering deserts to this cool, refreshing mountain perch. Something more than the inviting alpine environment can be found and experienced there. Rather than something an empiricist might put a finger on, it's more an evocative absence of something, such as the sound of silence that so unnerves city dwellers or the atmospheric vacuum left after a fast-moving storm.

Mornings and evenings are filled with this absence. The apprehension and anxiety that marbles my interior is gone then. It's a scary feeling not having the protection and comfort of my neuroses. The only thing I'm certain of is that this evocative absence does not want me to analyze it.

In a letter written at War Gods Spring to his friend Bill, Everett captured part of it:

> Dear Bill,
>
> A high wind is roaring in the tops of the tall pines. The moon is just rising on the rim of the desert, far below. Stars gleam through the pine boughs and the filmy clouds that move across the night sky. Graceful, slim-trunked aspens reach upward under the towering pines. Their slender, curving branches are white in the firelight, and an occasional downward breeze flickers their pale green leaves.
>
> The beauty of this place is perfect of its kind; I could ask for nothing more. A little spring trickles down under aspens and white fir. By day the marshy hollow is aswarm with gorgeous butterflies: Tiger and Zebra Swallowtails, the Angel Wings, the Mourning Cloak, and others. There are a hundred delightful places to sit and dream; friendly rocks to lean against—springy beds of pine needles to lie on and look up at the sky or the tall

smooth tree trunks, with spirals of branches and their tufted foliage. . . . No human comes to break the dreamy solitude. Far below, the tawny desert, seamed with canyons, throbs in the savage desert sun. But here it is lofty and cool.

The perfection of this place is one reason why I distrust ever returning to the cities. Here I wander in beauty and perfection. There one walks in the midst of ugliness and mistakes. All is made for man, but where can one find surroundings to match one's ideals and imaginings? It is possible to live and dream in ugly, ill-fitting places, but how much better to be where all is beautiful and unscarred.

The beauty of this country is becoming a part of me. I feel more detached from life and somehow gentler. Except for passing flurries, it has become impossible for me to censure anyone. I wish harm to no one and occasionally try to be kind, though it seems a futile striving. I have some good friends here, but no one who really understands why I am here or what I do. I don't know of anyone, though, who would have more than a partial understanding; I have gone too far alone.

Now the aspen trunks are tall and white in the moonlight. A wind croons in the pines. The mountain sleeps.

Peace to you,
Everett

In August of 1934, after camping at War God Springs, Everett descended the mountain and made his way around its south side to Endische Springs. From the springs he followed the famed Bernheimer Trail heading to Rainbow Bridge. My plan was to attempt to intersect Everett's route to Rainbow Bridge somewhere along the challenging trail blazed in 1922 by the Charles Bernheimer Expedition. While Everett went around the south side of Navajo Mountain, I chose another, highly unconventional and potentially much more dangerous route. I would proceed over the top of the mountain and then down its western slope; with luck I would intersect the Bernheimer somewhere along its twenty-mile length. I had no way of proving it, but I might have been the first and only person to ever attempt this route.

I did not expect to find clues about Everett's disappearance on my trek. I did, however, hope to better understand how Everett felt traveling alone for long periods in the natural world. For years, I have been fascinated by the month-long religious vision quests the Dineh take here. Like the Dineh and Everett but for reasons of my own, I would leave the turbulence of modern life behind and see just what was left of me.

THE BERNHEIMER EXPEDITIONS

The objective of the Charles Bernheimer expeditions was to discover an overland route to the magnificent Rainbow Bridge starting from the western side of Navajo Mountain. At the time, this route was thought to be impossible because of the difficult terrain. Its two expeditions in 1921 and 1922 caught the imagination of the world and focused the vision of dreamers and adventurers on the haunting beauty and impenetrable nature of this land. In 1921, with the assistance of famed Anglo guides John Wetherill and Zeke Johnson, the Bernheimer Expedition, which also included ten men and twice as many horses and mules, failed to find a westerly route to Rainbow Bridge or to circumvent the formidable Navajo Mountain. After nearly two months and countless attempts to discover a route, they conceded failure. There was no westerly route.

Bernheimer's exploits were published in his 1923 book, *Rainbow Bridge, Circling Navajo Mountain and Explorations in the "Bad Lands" of Southern Utah and Northern Arizona*, and exploits read like a classic eighteenth-century expedition into the darkest of Africa or into the freezing expanses of the poles. In all likelihood, Bernheimer and his men were the first whites to ever set foot on this stormy ocean of sandstone. Bernheimer's journal entries represent the first written documentation of the land, and he and his companions gave Anglo names to all the mesas, canyons, and plateaus.

Several years ago at the invitation of a pilot friend of mine, we flew over the area from Endische Springs to Rainbow Bridge. It resembled a twenty-five-square-mile sandstone labyrinth of fins, winding canyons, seams, crags, clefts, shelves, benches, tabletop plateaus, and swirling sandstone waves that washed up against the base of Navajo Mountain in torrents. From the ground, the labyrinth was foreboding. The landscape strips away depth and distance perception; it overwhelms adventurers with ever-rising and ever-receding fore- and backgrounds. This land has a way of surrounding and circling visitors into its cowlick-like centers. Time and again, Bernheimer struggled forward into dead ends where he and his men were forced to turn back, retracing the exact path out as they had followed in.

The next year, in July 1922, Bernheimer and company were back. Armed with the information they gathered on their first unsuccessful expedition, they slowly and methodically worked deep into the maze of sandstone again. They felt confident about success. Finally, after nearly two weeks, they stood at the last obstacle standing between them and the way down to Rainbow Bridge. At the top of a narrow canyon, which they named Rose Bud Canyon, the walls narrowed, then closed off completely. They could proceed no farther. But this time, instead of turning around and retreating, they used TNT to blast through the last 100 feet of sandstone, and in doing so, opened access to magnificent Rainbow Bridge.

Bernheimer lived in a time when vast tracts of the earth remained unexplored and environmental concerns did not extend to the land. The land was troublesome and men needed to change it, to mold it into environments that served them. This subordination of the land was part of the larger subordination that Victorian society imposed on all American ladies and gentlemen at the time.

A member of New York City's high society himself, Charles Bernheimer carried the banner of Victorian values into the wilderness. From his book, *Rainbow Bridge*: "In the early years of my Western travels I wore linen collars. They gave way to celluloid collars, which merely had to be wiped off with soap and water for cleansing. Soft collars followed; finally the coloured cotton bandana replaced all others (not the silk sort, which we associate with the toilet of cowboys and Western frontiersmen). These I found served the purpose admirably."

The Bernheimer Trail is seldom used anymore. Only the strongest and best prepared make the trek. Each mile of the trail was paid for with the lives of the horses and mules who were worked unmercifully, and who either plummeted off cliffs or who went without water for so long, they keeled over dead.

I had no idea of how or where I would find the Bernheimer Trail, but one thing was certain: my pathway over the crest of the mountain was no cakewalk. In 1921 Bernheimer and John Wetherill hiked to the top of Navajo Mountain, hoping to find a way down to Rainbow Bridge, but on arrival at the summit they concluded it was impossible.

Though I was pressed to my physical limit, the first day out was delightful, and the sun and I worked slowly over the crest of the mountain and down its western slope. My load was far too heavy, and I couldn't shake my anxiety about traveling alone. If something were to happen to me, there was no chance I would be helped or, perhaps, ever seen again.

From the crest of Navajo Mountain, or *Nasstsis'aan*—which means in Dineh, the Head of Earth Women,—the burning, upside-down desert of the Escalante Drainage to the north was spectacular. I could not imagine a more sublime view anywhere on earth. Hidden somewhere within the deep and winding canyons far below, Everett's songs and poems, his hopes and dreams were still alive. They echoed up out of the canyons and onto the great Fifty Mile Ridge plateau where the wind carried them in all four directions.

Looking down on the Escalante Drainage from the mountain's high slopes, Charles Bernheimer wrote:

> *. . . we were high above the country to the north and our view was unobstructed for miles and the San Juan River was easily visible. The colouring of the landscape suggested the hues found in petrified wood. The baldheaded domes of the slick-rocks stood out sharply, surrounded by the flat tops of mesas separated by the dark, vein-like burrowings of minor canyons. The purple shades cast at random by floating clouds, the iridescence of distant mountain ranges, and the deep turquoise sky filled heart and mind with rapture over the glory of this Wonderland.*

From the mountaintop, I dropped into forests of Engelmann spruce, aspen and ponderosa, jack, red and yellow pines. I discovered secret meadows and gardens of colorful wildflowers growing along creeks and brooks. I worked around impassible rock piles and discovered hidden ponds and small lakes made by beaver.

At sundown, I made camp, and as I did, the wind rushed through the pines. An apparition hovered at the edge of the grove. Before I could get a good look, it vanished. Everett's lust for life enveloped me here. I sensed he was not so very far ahead of me. I felt close to him and somehow closer to myself. Late that night, I was awakened by a hard rainfall, yet I remained safe and dry, protected under the giant boughs of a ponderosa. Later, I was awakened again, this time by a tremendous shaking under me.

Earthquake! I sat up at attention, listening for the sound of rocks coming down from above. I scanned the ponderosa with my flashlight, hoping it wouldn't topple over and crush me. After a long time—I don't know how long—I fell back to sleep.

The next morning everything was soaked. The mountain air was delicious and filled with the fragrance of pine. After coffee and a good deal of lounging around, I loaded my backpack and worked west. Within an hour, my progress was slowed to a crawl as the terrain became extremely difficult. To the right and below me, the alpine carpet had eroded away dramatically; enormous pieces of the mountain had sloughed off, disappearing into the deep, multicolored canyons far below.

Hiking near the erosion zone could be very dangerous, and the weight of a single man might be enough to make the ground give way, so I cautiously worked westward, attempting to maintain a longitudinal line a hundred feet or so above the slide area. Unfortunately, time and time again, the steep terrain drew me down close to the edge. I felt my strength slip away against the impossible terrain and the weight of my pack. I gave way a few feet at a time, and a growing sense of danger enveloped me.

Ahead of me a low ridge rose up and blocked my view. I moved cautiously toward the ridge, checking often to make sure I was a safe distance above the erosion zone. Finally, after struggling through a dangerous rock pile to the ridge crest, I was aghast at what I found! The mountain on the other side of the ridge was gone! An enormous shelf of mountain starting hundreds of feet above me had been jettisoned! The exposed gash was twenty feet deep at its center and five hundred feet across. All that remained were a few rocks, severed roots, and the dirt that had not seen the light of day for eons, if ever. Adding to my horror, the grasses and roots at the landslide's edge were green and appeared to have been torn very recently.

Suddenly, it dawned on me! The rumbling the night before! It was the mountainside cutting loose under the weight of the rain and sliding away.

The ground shuddered slightly, so I quickly moved away from the edge. Turning to plot my retreat, I saw that I had unwittingly hiked down onto a rain-soaked peninsula. The peninsula was surrounded by the erosion that was eating away the mountainside. I stood on the only piece of lush mountain slope that had not slipped away. The only route to safety was to thread a path back across the rain-soaked alpine carpet, then hike straight up until I was well above the peninsula and the danger zone. At any moment the appendage could break away and slide into oblivion, taking me with it. Despite this or perhaps because of it, a numbing exhaustion overtook me. I had to sit and rest. Catch my breath. Calm myself.

Two hours later I was high above the danger zone, sitting on the edge of a plateau that hid a small beautiful lake. I would go no farther today. My legs refused commands and my arms and hands were trembling. It is a shame there are so few occasions when we must push ourselves past the point of exhaustion to the place our mortality can be viewed. Perhaps if I visited this place more often, my senses might be awakened, enhanced, enlivened, and somehow more completed. My search for Everett had taken me to this place twice so far—this time, and once far below on the burning plateau above Davis Gulch with Don, Thelma, Kathrine, and Helen.

By facing nature, and in some cases the possibility of death, Everett made himself available for attachment as few people do. To a real extent, nature asks me to open my heart wider than it's ever been before, softening the judging and moralizing that at times has characterized my behavior. In solitude, there is time for me to embrace the contradictions and paradoxes of life and of death. Conflict, discussion, and reconciliation have a venue there that enable me to reattach to the deeper meanings of my life. The genuine odyssey or quest is not about piling up miles or dangerous experiences. It is a deeply felt, risky, and unpredictable tour of the soul. The search for Everett helps me find the courage to embark on this difficult path again and again.

After a restful nap on the hard-as-hell rocks, I floated naked on my back in the cold, teardrop-shaped lake. Later, I sat at the edge of the plateau and surveyed the Escalante Drainage and Glen Canyon far below. Few mortals have seen it as I did that day. As I followed the outline of Glen Canyon, now filled with the waters of the Colorado and San Juan Rivers to form Lake Powell, I could not shake a feeling of being cheated. The waters of the lake have risen into the surrounding canyon systems, offering them up to anyone with a powerboat. Only a few generations ago, these canyons were the most remote places on the face of the earth—the Bernheimer Expeditions exemplified this. As it is today, anyone with a powerboat can bring the devaluation of easy access to all of these natural places.

Ed Abbey's voice from his book, *Desert Solitaire*, floated on the air:

> *Wilderness is not a luxury. Wilderness is a necessity of the human spirit, as vital to our lives as water and good bread. A civilization which destroys what little remains of the wild, the sparse, the original, cuts itself off from its origins and betrays the principles of civilization itself. Our love of wilderness is more than a hunger for what is always beyond our reach; it is an expression of loyalty to the earth, the earth which bore us and sustains us, the only home we shall ever know, the only paradise we ever need.*

Abbey spoke passionately about access to the wilderness. He believed half the beauty of the wilderness lay in its remoteness and in its relative difficulty of access. When the difficulty of access, to wilderness is removed by building roads or by motorboat travel, as in the case of Lake Powell, an integral element in its magic is removed. "Nature becomes no more than isolated geological oddities when it is easy to access; it is reduced to an extension of that museum-like diorama to which industrial tourism tends to reduce the natural world."

The next morning my strength had returned, yet the path was no less difficult than the day before. I passed from the alpine into the subalpine and then into the domain of the high-forested sandstone desert. I labored down into deep oxide-colored ravines of purple and blue and aqua; then under the weight of my pack, I struggled up the other side and out again, only to find myself just a few hundred feet farther along than before. Again and again, I found and then lost what I believed might be a way off the mountain and onto the Bernheimer Trail. One of the many canyons below would lead off the mountain, but I had no idea which one it was; all the rest led to impossible narrows, dead ends, and cliffs from which I would be forced to retreat—if possible.

By early afternoon, I was at a point where I could study the jumble of swale-like crags and swirling sandstone formations that hid Rainbow Bridge below. I grew tired and frustrated. The farther I went, the more impossible my route became. I decided to camp on a small flat plateau where the ground was soft, and I had a tremendous view to the west. The next morning I left my backpack behind and searched all day for a way off the mountain. No luck. I camped that night at my previous night's campsite.

In the morning, I neatly folded my topographical maps and placed them in my backpack. They would do me no good here; the topography is so broken, my maps couldn't chart an accurate path. Somewhere below I threw caution to the wind and entered the labyrinth. The morning passed slowly into afternoon as I worked back and forth downward, exploring the tops of many dangerous-looking canyons.

To the west was No Name Mesa, connected to the mountain by a narrow neck of sandstone with sheer cliffs on either side. The mesa rose above the rest of the labyrinth and was covered with juniper and sage. It appeared that I could easily cross from the mountain onto the mesa, but from my vantage point it looked as though the mesa would be just as difficult to get off of as the mountain. I turned north and hiked for about a half hour before seeing a large formation of fins below and to the northwest. I decided this was the place I would head down but not before a good night's sleep.

The next day I headed straight down into the maze. Descending between the walls of the canyon, the rocky terrain under my feet turned into deep orange-colored sand, sometimes reaching all the way to mid-calf. The farther I proceeded, the narrower the canyon became until it was only a few feet wide. It was so steep that without the sand cementing my legs down, I would not have been able to stand upright. Resting in the shade, I drank water and acknowledged to myself that I would never be able to climb back out. The combination of the weight of my pack, the deep sand, and the canyon's tortuous descent meant I had only one escape option: forward. For some reason, this acknowledgment did not frighten me. I had committed to this route and felt good about my decision. I had reached the point where I would face whatever the land had in store for me.

At the bottom of the canyon, I discovered I was at the mouth of a sandstone cul-de-sac with walls towering fifty feet above me. Upon venturing into the cul-de-sac to investigate, I spotted one wall that might be scalable. After scratching and clawing my way up to its saddle, I saw the fins I had seen from far above. Good, I thought. Though I had no good reason to be comforted, I remembered that the Bernheimer Expedition was ultimately forced to use explosives to blast an opening through a group of fins, allowing the trail to Rainbow Bridge to be blazed. Maybe these were the same fins.

Between me and the fins was a winding canyon that I must find my way down through. The canyon contained a number of deep and narrow sections, each with a nasty plunge pool hidden from my vision. I moved forward, finding each section negotiable with care and effort. At the bottom, I worked my way between two enormous fins. After a while, the passageway widened and, thankfully, the going became easier for about a mile. The narrows were haunting and cool. Occasionally, I could glimpse the tops of the ridges, perhaps 300 feet above.

Slowly at first, almost imperceptibly, the fins narrowed and began to close in on me until I was forced to take my pack off and pull it behind me. Up ahead several hundred yards, it appeared that the fins closed off completely, making them impassable. I feared that, like the Bernheimer Expeditions, I had worked my way into one of the hundreds of dead ends in this maze and would be forced to turn back.

But turn back to what and where? I couldn't climb back out the way I came in, even if I could find the exact place I descended—which I was not certain I could do. I felt claustrophobic. I had been at the bottom of this narrow canyon far too long.

Reaching the point where the two fins rose up and appeared to close off, I discovered that one fin was broken away at its base. Its rough edges appeared as if it had been blasted away. On the opposite wall, someone had scrolled something in the sandstone. I couldn't make any of it out, but there were dates and several sets of initials. I closed my eyes and let my fingertips move over the stone as if I could read braille, but I can't so it was no use. Time and the elements work slowly in nature, but they never take a day off. Could I have stumbled onto one of the places the Bernheimer Expedition blasted, I wondered? I stood there for a long time, imagining Charles Bernheimer and his men standing there in this exact spot so many years before me.

On the other side of the fins I dropped into a secret valley and discovered it filled with the mythic purple sage! I had never seen anything like it. Though I had no idea where I was, I had the sensation of arriving at some predestined destination. I sat down in the shadow of the purple sage and quickly fell asleep.

At twilight, an unholy saffron radiated off the sandstone and gathered like mist in the eddies and the low places. In one of these low places in 1922, Charles Bernheimer, too, discovered a colony of the exceptionally rare purple sage. He wrote:

> *Purple sage grows in the crevices of these Baldheads. I also found it in the rocks at the easterly gateway of Surprise Valley,*

at the foot of a cliff ruin near by. I am told that it is to be found nowhere else, except in Kaibito. It blooms in May. This lonely messenger of joyful repose, dark purple blossom with an orange centre, modestly peeping out of the cracks of its salmon-coloured rock home, thrills the traveller as does the edelweiss of the Swiss Alps.

I was glad when night fell. I had lost my ability to differentiate between sandstone and sky. The seam running between heaven and earth had simply disappeared. I had never experienced this phenomenon before. Luckily, the sky was filled with stars. A sense of well-being swept over me, a sense of peace and wholeness I've never felt in any city. Nature helps disintegrate the layers of confusion and somehow allows me to reconnect the outer and inner worlds of my existence. I cooked a simple meal of dehydrated pasta and tomato sauce over my C2 gas stove but fell soundly asleep before I could finish it.

In the morning, after making my way into another canyon, I discovered a trail marked with cairns. The trail bore the prints of hiking boots. Nearly ten days had elapsed since I'd left the modern world behind, and to be standing on a man-made trail again made me feel strange and resentful. As I studied the footprints the way an archaeologist might, a group of hikers appeared before me. They wore sunglasses, had cameras hanging from straps around their necks, and only a few of them carried water. Their tidiness was incongruent and looked terribly uncomfortable.

You are not responsible for these people, I said to myself.

Thankfully, among the group was a man in his fifties; he wore leather hiking boots, had a large canteen, and doffed an African pith helmet, which he tipped in my direction. He was obviously their guide.

"Where are you coming from, might I ask?" he inquired, a British accent tainting his words.

"War God Springs, my good man," I said slightly mocking. "Navajo Mountain." I wiped the sweat and dirt from my brow, spit on the ground between us, and pointed to the mountain behind me.

"Good god, man! Are you serious?" he asked, his wry smile expanding wider and wider.

I nodded to the pathway before me. "The Bernheimer Trail, I presume?"

"Why, yes! Yes, indeed," he said. "And you, my good fellow, must be Dr. Livingston, I presume?"

THE BERKELEY EXPEDITION

In late August, Everett linked up with an archaeological expedition from the University of California and the University of Northern Arizona. The expedition was exploring cave dwellings along the Utah and Arizona strip, cataloging what members found. After nearly three months of solitary wandering, Everett was happy for the opportunity—if only for a week or two—to live and work with a group of young men. It was to be one of his last opportunities to share the company of contemporaries.

Though Everett traveled alone, he was definitely not a loner. He was not out in the wilderness to get away from people, nor did he avoid them when their paths crossed. If Everett saw smoke rising from a campfire, he would turn his burros and head that way. People who knew him remembered the same thing: Everett was friendly and enjoyed spending time with others.

The idea of a traveling companion was a frequent subject of Everett's letters. He discussed its merits and drawbacks, but he did not waiver in his belief that no companion was better than a poor or unsuitable one. Everett was fearful that if he did find a traveling companion, he would ultimately be rejected for his oddity and eccentricity. Far too often, he concluded that few people truly understood him, yet he still longed for that special sharing of experience companions can bring.

With the Berkeley expedition, Everett served as an unpaid cook, receiving his meals as payment. He was excited about his new friends and learned much about the ancient Indians who once lived here. Although he wrote kindly of his new friends, their recollections of him indicated a more reserved and introspective person. While they considered him friendly, he is remembered as quiet and strange.

Everett was part of a group who separated from the main expedition and traveled to a remote and difficult cave where they discovered the mummified remains of two people. The group spent nearly two weeks camping at the cave, and one of his companions remembered that while they worked long hours, Everett sat near the cave's entrance or on a nearby cliff edge, gazing out over the canyons below as if in a daydream.

It is possible that while the archaeologists and their youthful helpers worked away inside the cave, Everett was working hard, too—digging down into the sands of his own archaeology. In a way, we are all on a personal archaeological dig. The mysterious sands of our existence possess more than just an accumulation of our years and experiences. They also possess much more than our intellect can possibly account for. The reasons we dig and what we expect to find buried within our archaeology are not clear.

If we are brave and persistent as Everett was and if we dig down carefully one stratum at a time, we will find the ideas and dreams we lost or discarded there. This debris is a treasure of great value. This deeply personal archaeological dig is a dirty and difficult work. I believe few people do this work, fearing they might find only emptiness and pain. Perhaps Brigham Atene was right: our souls have no home so we deny much about our true nature. In a way, a malaise of great proportions has swept across our cultural landscape. The writer Walter Lippman, in his 1930s book *Whirl the King*, explained that after the inhumane Victorian moral values of the late nineteenth century were overthrown and replaced by intellectual pursuit, our society fell into chaos [Whirl] and we have been lost ever since. Lippman did not advocate a return to Victorian morality but wrote that what replaced it was a numbing confusion: no one seemed to know who he or she was or where she or he was going. "People race from one fad to another, from one headline sensation to the next, hoping to find the answer to their lostness, and when they find nothing, they race on in a whirl," Lippman wrote.

Today, Lippman's analysis seems prophetic. We live in an intellectual and technological paradise but a moral and social quagmire. I believe that since the mid-1970s there has been a slow, confused, mindless drift back to a kind of pseudo-Victorian moral posture. Still, many people—myself included —reject this proposition and have set out in search of answers to the deeper questions of our lives. In Gretel Ehrlich's book, *The Solace of Open Spaces*, which is about the power of silence and nature, she laments, "The shrill estrangement some of us felt in our twenties has been replaced a decade or so later by a hangdog, collective blues. With our burgeoning careers and families, we want to join up but it's difficult to know how or where. . . . Now, with our senses enlivened—because that is the only context we have to go by—we hook change onto change ad nauseum."

Of the young men Everett worked with during the Berkeley expedition, most grew into men, raised families, had long and fulfilling careers, retired, and have since died. The archaeology of their lives is similar to ours with one important exception: most of them had fathers and strong male examples from which to pattern their lives.

It has been three generations since the fathers, uncles, grandfathers, and old male initiators disappeared from the family circle. When we look along our archaeological pathways, few of us find signs that good strong men walked there. Once, boys stood next to their fathers out on the land and in the farm fields; men of all ages worked together. Many social scientists believe that the industrial revolution took the men away from their families and put them into factories. Nothing has been the same since. Once, it took a young man until age twenty-five before reaching maturity; now it could take that same person until he is age forty or fifty. Sadly, many girls grow into women without ever experiencing the beautiful energy of a mature, healthy man.

In this poem excerpt, the famed Spanish poet Antonio Machado speaks of the tremendous loss men and women have suffered.

The wind one brilliant day
Called to my soul with the odor of
Jasmine and said,
In return for the odor of my jasmine
I'd like the odor of your roses.
But I have no roses, I answered,
All the flowers in my garden are dead.
The wind then said,
I'll take all the withered petals and
Yellow leaves, and the wind left—
And I wept. And I said to myself,
"What have you done with the garden that
Has been entrusted to you?"

HOPI LAND

After leaving the Berkeley expedition, Everett worked east to Hopi land where he wanted to witness the tribe's annual August dances.

I arrived on Hopi land for the first time in 1982 in the late afternoon. Black-bottomed clouds moved quickly over the land as if not wanting to linger. The desolation was complete: it is a barren, featureless, windswept place. Hopi land does not beckon one forward, and the horizons fall away in all directions as if turning their backs to outsiders.

At the center of this unremarkable landscape, three puny mesas peek out above the rest. I had read about the three-fingered Hopi mesas, and when they finally came into view on the eastern horizon, I was disappointed. Since the Hopis are considered to be the most peace-loving and deeply religious people on earth, not to mention one of the most secretive, I somehow had envisioned a spectacular geography to go along with it, something along the lines of the temples and escarpments found in the Valley of the Gods north of Monument Valley.

Bask—the wonder dog—and I had been on the road for a week. We had gone from place to place, camping and hiking. Nearing First Mesa, I spotted the ancient stone houses of Old Oraibi perched on the cliff above. As the highway winds closer to the mesa, the Stone Age dwellings are at times clearly visible with varying levels of detail, or they are dissolving either partially or completely until they merge back into the cliff face and disappear as if they never existed at all. It reminded me of the Hopi legend of Kowawa, the mythic village that is always there on the distant horizon.

Anglo anthropologists believe that hundreds of years ago, the Hopi were driven from their homes and took refuge on the mesa tops. From the mesas the nonviolent Hopi could see invaders and could protect themselves. They hoped the ghastly emptiness of their new surroundings would collapse the raspy lung of further intrusion. This theory may well be correct, but the Hopi legend of creation tells another story. After Tiowa—The Creator—destroyed the first three paradises he had created for man, he built the Fourth World, the desolate world of today. Tiowa was forced to destroy the previous three paradise worlds because life was so easy that people became lazy, corrupt, and evil. When Tiowa set man down on the Fourth World, the people were surprised to find a barren and inhospitable land. Here, man was forced to work and make great sacrifices just to survive. Here, man did not become lazy or corrupt. Here, man listened for the voice of Tiowa through the soft spot on the top of his head and stayed pure through prayer.

When we finally crested the steep road to the top of First Mesa, a sign welcomed us: Old Oraibi next right. Old Oraibi is the oldest continuously occupied community in North America, dating back some 800 years. I strained to get a look but all I could see was a collection of low, ramshackle stone houses, backlit by a brazen red sunset that was punching holes in some hostile-looking clouds on the horizon.

Turning off the paved highway, I was surprised to find that no road leads to the village. Instead, tire tracks run across the hardened earth in all directions. I could chose my own path. Neutral. No golden arches, no "gas and go" flashing lights to mark my way. The tawdry commercialism that distinguishes my culture was absent. Though my destination was clearly visible just a few thousand feet away, I was lost.

Finally, I proceeded as an adventurer—half frightened by what might be in store, half drawn forward by some inexplicable force. At a group of tiny, one-roomed, Stone Age houses, I was suddenly transported away, back in time. It was Tasupi, or sunset time as the Hopi call it, and Old Oraibi was a prehistoric twilight zone.

"We are in another time and place," I muttered, more to myself than to Bask.

I felt truly alive. Every muscle, corpuscle, electron, and atom within me was jumping for joy.

I sat bug-eyed for a long time. After a while my attention was drawn to a group of boys playing with a football. I drove cross-country and stopped to ask for directions to a gas station. The boys did not answer my question; instead, they stared into the backseat where Bask stood majestically, gazing back at them.

"Is he brave?" a beautiful, bright-faced Hopi boy finally asked.

No one had ever inquired about Bask's bravery before. Anglo children invariably ask the same two questions, "Does he bite?" or "Is he mean?"

"Yes." I said, proudly. "He is brave."

Another boy asked, "Would he fight a mountain lion?"

"Well, I'm not really sure, but I'd bet he would fight a mountain lion to save me. He would lay his life down for me."

The boys smiled, nodded approval, and looked at one another in agreement. They had small rounded faces, thick shiny hair, smooth soft-looking skin, and perfect white teeth.

"Yes," the bright-faced boy said, "he is brave!"

Without taking their eyes from Bask, the group pointed in the direction of the gas station. I drove on slowly, making my way around low, squat houses built hundreds of years before the Europeans arrived with their predilection for town squares and linear uniformity. I moved closer to the cliff edge and farther back in time. As I came within sight of the cliff, I spotted an eight-foot-tall, cone-shaped, antique gas pump. I had never seen one like it except in old photographs.

The antique gas pump reminded me of Robbie the Robot from the 1950s science-fiction film. Standing in front of the only structure that appeared to have been built this millennium, Robbie saluted me. On one side, the nozzle and hose arced upward in a salute; on the other side, a long, manual pump handle pointed downward. The top one-third of the cone-shaped pump was made of clear glass; this glass reservoir held perhaps five gallons and was filled with gasoline. The dying embers of Tasupi caught the gasoline in the glass container, and Robbie the Robot's head came alive, glowing and radiating as if possessed by the magic of the ages.

I was back in Hopi land again, driving to Mishongnovi to meet with an artist whose mother knew Everett. Passing the turnoff to Old Oraibi, I couldn't help but think about the group of boys who were so taken by Bask. Enough time has passed since our meeting that they had grown into young men. The pathway from boyhood to manhood for the Hopi is directed by the elders in accordance with ancient, time-honored religious rituals. Hopi boys walk the same exact path to manhood as did their fathers, grandfathers, great-grandfathers, and great-great-grandfathers.

In the Washing-of-the-Hair ritual, all boys deemed worthy are initiated into manhood. Little is known about this initiation rite, but what is known is that the Hopi gods and their earthly emissaries, the living Taalawtumsi deities, oversee it. The Taalawtumsi deities are wooden icons named Dawn Woman, Corn Maiden (a kind Hopi mother earth), her husband, and their daughter. Carved from ancient cottonwood tree roots, these centuries-old icons are at the heart of the Hopi religion. The Taalawtumsi are as sacred to the Hopi as the Koran is to the Arabs, the Talmud to the Jews, and the Bible to the Christians.

When Everett wandered onto the three mesas with his burros, the Hopi saw something special in him. They invited Everett to dance with them in the Antelope Dance. This invitation is puzzling because it came at a time when the Hopi were about to close their sacred August dances to all outsiders. The Hopi had been imposed upon enough, and they no longer wanted outsiders to even see the dances let alone participate in them. Not only was Everett invited to dance but the normally shy and aloof Hopi showered him with friendship, mementos, and love.

On August 25, Everett wrote to his parents: "Yesterday I saw the Snake dance here, and now it is beginning to rain. I have been having great fun with the Hopis here, and just finished a painting of the village. The children were clustered all around me, some helping and some hindering . . ."

I like to think that the Hopi invited Everett to dance with them to give him strength. The Hopi could see that Everett was making two separate but interwoven passages all alone. The first passage is the one that transforms boys into men. The second is the journey from the outside of his life—overcoming society's demands and the whirl of our lost society—to the inside of his life; that is, the movement toward the deep discovery or rediscovery of one's true nature. Perhaps the Hopi even knew that Everett's days were numbered, so they embraced him because they are a compassionate people.

The reason I have not been able to get the Hopi boys out of my mind lately is that the Washing of the Hair ceremony, the ritual initiating Hopi boys into manhood, was cancelled in the late eighties. For the first time in hundreds of years, the ceremony was postponed—indefinitely. No Hopi boy will become a man until the ceremony is performed once again.

In what has become known as one of the most devastating religious thefts in modern history, cowboy grave robbers stole Dawn Woman and the other sacred living Taalawtumsi from their home in a secret cave where they have lived for nearly four centuries. The Hopi religion is so secretive that, were it not for the thefts of the icons, the outside world would have never known that the Taalawtumsi even existed.

The importance of this loss cannot be assessed by outsiders. A Hopi friend told me, "The Taalawtumsi are living deities, not wooden idols. To my people, the Taalawtumsi are alive just as you and I are alive and standing here right now."

From what little is known, the living Taalawtumsi lead the secret Washing of the Hair initiation ceremony as well as many other ceremonies in the Hopis' ancient religion. Their disappearance means that boys cannot be initiated into manhood, and if there are no men to perform the religious ceremonies, the religion itself is threatened with extinction. One Hopi told me, "We are a tree without its roots."

In 1991, the truth—or part of it—about what happened to the Taalawtumsi finally became known. Told to investigators by a man who believed he was the victim of a curse because of his involvement in the theft—a curse that ultimately made him come forward and confess—this is the tragic story:

> The Taalawtumsi were taken by two Anglo cowboys late one night as they searched Hopi land for ancient ruins and burial mounds to rob. Finding the Taalawtumsi resting in their hidden cave and realizing they were into something big, the two cowboys took the icons and attempted to sell them in Flagstaff, Arizona. The thieves were unsuccessful, partly because they were not trusted but primarily because even Hopi experts and knowledgeable collectors had no idea what the priceless objects really were.

> Sometime later, the Taalawtumsi were sold to a third man who paid very little for them and who kept them for a number of years until he became worried he was about to be arrested. Because of this fear, the man claims he chopped the Taalawtumsi into pieces with an axe and burned them as fuel in his woodstove.

The Hopi reeled when they heard the news. How can this be? they asked. Who would do such a thing? But remarkably, just as despair descended over the tribe, the Hopi religious elders living high atop First Mesa came forward. The Taalawtumsi have not been destroyed, they said. They are alive and well! The elders told fellow tribesmen that the Taalawtumsi were calling out to them. One traditional leader told me, "They cry out and plead for help, 'Come and rescue us. We were not destroyed. Come and get us,' they tell us."

Whether the Taalawtumsi were destroyed or survive yet, calling out for someone to come rescue them as the traditional religious leaders insist, the Hopi people are without their living deities. This thoughtful and prayerful people are struggling to figure out what to do. The heart of their age-old religion has been ripped out, and no boys will become men because of the greed and stupidity of the two cowboys.

This is not the first blow the Hopi have been forced to endure at the hands of outsiders. Perhaps most important and troubling among them is the ongoing Hopi-Navajo Land Dispute.

The encroachment of the Navajo onto Hopi land started 250 years ago, before the United States of America was formed, and it continues today. On sixteen occasions since the administration of Abraham Lincoln, presidents have issued executive orders taking Hopi land away from them and giving it to the much larger and more aggressive Navajo. To date, this land grab has cost the Hopi 80 percent of its territory and is known as the Hopi-Navajo Land Dispute.

The Hopi are a reasonable people, but they are running scared. One morning a Hopi friend of mine, Alan Sekaquptewa, and I stood at the cliff edge on First Mesa.

"Look," Alan said, pointing northwest, "over there. See those tin roofs reflecting the sun?"

I shaded my eyes with my hand and squinted, "Yes, I can see them."

"They are Navajo houses," Alan said in disgust. "We can see them from here, and they can see us." Sekaquptewa turned in a circle with his arms outstretched. "Once, all this land—as far as you can see—was Hopi land. But now, we are surrounded. They will not be happy until they have all the land, and we are no more. We are peaceful, but what are we to do?"

Few dispute that aboriginal Hopi land contained more than eight million acres of desert, mountain, and canyon country, yet today the homeland has been pared down to 550,000 acres. The Hopi now live on an island of land surrounded by the Navajo nation. In 1974, Congress settled the land dispute once and for all when it enacted the Hopi-Navajo Land Settlement

Act. This act divided the disputed territory and drew new borders. While the Hopi were unhappy with the settlement act, they were pleased that finally they would receive justice. No more land would be stolen from them. On the other hand, the Navajo refused to give up some of the lands agreed to, and so twenty years later the negotiations continue. Incidentally, the most hotly disputed area is Big Mountain, the place where Nat and Alice Tahonnie live and where their family has resided for 200 years.

Since my first visits to the mesas, I have seen a change in the Hopi people. They are less friendly and more suspicious. The Hopi have their backs to the wall and after hundreds of years of nonviolence, the Hopi are determined to fight if necessary to protect what is left.

"We are afraid," Sekaquptewa told me. "What will become of us?"

I was ashamed and could only shrug my shoulders and push the dirt around my feet into little piles.

"The Navajo want to assimilate us. They want to swallow us up and make us Dineh," Sekaquptewa said angrily.

Assimilation. This sounds familiar. Alan Sekaquptewa sounds like Nat Tahonnie and Brigham Atene. The Dineh will ingest and assimilate the Hopi, and the American culture will ingest and assimilate the Dineh.

Who or what will ingest and assimilate us?

The next morning I visited the house of a well-known Hopi artist, and after greeting me, she led me to the back of her house. Smiling, she pointed to an old drawing hanging on the back wall. I moved closer to take a look. It was an original sketch by Everett of Second Mesa. It was unframed, and its edges were frayed and curled by time.

"It has been hanging here since my grandmother traded it for a small bowl," the artist said. "It is one of his best."

Once again, the distance between Everett and I compressed. I was hot on his trail. I thought to myself, Run out of the house and down the highway after him. If you run fast enough, you will surely catch him.

THE TERRELL EXPEDITION

When reporter John Terrell and Captain Neal Johnson reached Dunn's Trading Post at the remote outpost of Navajo Mountain, most of the residents of the small community were waiting for them. A Navajo elder once told me, "News travels quickly in Navajo land. A baby can be born in the north today, and everyone in the south will know about it tomorrow."

In 1935, Anglos were still a rare sight, especially white men searching for a dead man. Even more fascinating to the residents of the remote community was the black box camera that the white men carried with them. Some of those waiting for the pair had traveled from far out on the land just to see the camera. They believed the box could steal their spirit. When Terrell saw all the people standing around on his arrival, he quickly retrieved the camera to take some pictures, but everyone scattered, leaving him standing there alone. Terrell learned that if he wanted information, it was best to give people a quick glimpse of the camera then put it away.

Among the Dineh at the trading post was Dougi, the famous tracker. Dougi stepped forward and introduced himself. He knew they needed a tracker and that they were looking for him. Dougi would track Everett if Terrell's camera was left behind. Reluctantly, Terrell agreed, and no photographs of Dougi or what they found in Davis Gulch exists.

The next day, the three men left Navajo Mountain on horseback. Dougi led the two Anglos north from the mountain into canyon country to a place a few miles east of the confluence of the San Juan and the Colorado Rivers. They followed an ancient Anasazi pathway that the Navajo used when traveling north to Escalante to trade with whites. From Terrell's report, "It was magnificent country; in part, thick forest, elsewhere bare red rock, sweeps of green pinion, vast reaches of sage. The sacred mountain crossed, we looked upon a world resembling an endless tossing red and yellow sea, still turbulent after being stirred to its depths by a great storm."

After fording the dangerous San Juan and Colorado Rivers, they worked several miles north over Wilson Mesa to the Escalante River and then onto

Davis Gulch. Over the next several days, Dougi found many clues overlooked by the three previous searches. He even found Everett's footprints at the base of Fifty Mile Ridge. Because of this it was later speculated that Everett climbed Fifty Mile Ridge, made camp there, and returned his burros to Davis Gulch where they were found by searchers.

When Dougi concluded his search, he was stumped. In the concluding installment of John Terrell's four-part series, he reported:

> We set Dougi to working on the trail out of Davis Canyon. His final verdict was: "White boy come in, not go out."
>
> "You mean he didn't walk or ride out?" I asked.
>
> Dougi stared at me, fear plainly visible in his obsidian eyes. I understood what he meant.
>
> Then Ruess was buried somewhere here, we concluded.
>
> "No grave. Could find," Dougi said.
>
> I inquired if it was possible that Ruess could have gone down the river on a raft . . . to his death.
>
> "Raft and packs would float," was Dougi's quiet reply, and we saw the wisdom in this conclusion. The river is closely watched at such places as Lee's Ferry. Then Dougi added a final blow to this speculation, abruptly halting it.
>
> "Only few places where raft could be made. Me went there, look. No raft made."

So then, Everett went into Davis Gulch and left no trace of departing. The quasi-searches at the time and the subsequent searches by people such as me have turned up nothing new in or around Davis Gulch and tend to confirm Dougi's mysterious conclusion.

After returning to Navajo Mountain, Terrell visited another important Navajo, Hosteen Geishi. Geishi and his clan lived in the area south of the two rivers where they hunted and raised horses. Geishi had twenty riders who worked the only area where Everett could have crossed into Navajo land. "I know every man in the country," Geishi told them, "and everyone who passes through. We see them all and know their business. Everett did not come this way."

After searching for weeks and interviewing many Dineh, Terrell ended his inquiry. He concluded his four-part story this way: "This is the result: Everett Ruess was murdered in the vicinity of Davis Canyon. His valuable outfit was stolen. He never reached the Colorado River. . . . But some day, pieces of his outfit will turn up. Then we shall take to the trail again."

The Terrell Expedition is noteworthy for eliminating the possibility that

Everett crossed the San Juan and Colorado Rivers and entered Navajo country. He learned it was impossible for a white man to travel onto Navajo land without someone knowing about it. There is no way of testing the veracity of Dougi and the others who Terrell depended upon. It remains a real possibility that Everett's demise was at the hand of a Navajo, and the identity of the killer has been kept secret within the tribe, ultimately dying with the last survivors of the knowledge.

The more I investigated, the more troubled I became about Dougi and his involvement with the search to find Everett. Dougi was in Escalante at the same time as Everett. People in Escalante reported seeing Everett sitting in the shade of a cottonwood tree with three Navajos on November 10, the day before he left town. Dougi was one of those Navajos. Days later, Dougi returned to Navajo land via the same Hole in the Rock road Everett took. After Everett's disappearance was discovered, Dougi told authorities that as he traveled south on the Hole in the Rock Trail, he passed three Navajos who were traveling north to Escalante. Dougi gave the impression that one of these men hated whites and was capable of murder.

I arrived at the Grand Canyon's South Rim after dark and camped in the overflow area of an expansive campground. The overflow sat on a slight incline above the main campground, which is situated in a deep depression or bowl. From my campsite I could see dozens of campfires dotting the forest below. An amorphous cloud of blue-gray smoke hung above the bowl, its finger-like tentacles intertwining the tops of the ponderosa pines like some insidious cancer. The cloud pulsed with a dull light as though it possessed a heart beating somewhere deep within.

Nearby, the shadows of my neighbors were cast outward by their campfires. I mused that if my neighbors could just see how much enjoyment their shadows had dancing and cavorting, they might not stand around the campfire like objects of great weight and volume. To my left, flashlights moved from one place to another without apparent rhythm or discernible reason. Somewhere off in the distance, laughter was carried to me on the cool night air. The voices were happy and rose up in utter satisfaction of living. From a nearby campsite, a child called out, "Mommie." A sweet reply returned in German, "Night, babe."

I spread my tarp, arranged my sleeping bag, and collapsed into it. It had been a long day and it felt good to stretch out on the ground and sleep. Sometime later I awoke; there were no sounds and everything was peaceful. The campfires had died out and everyone slept. Starlight filtered through the filigree of pine boughs above, gently swaying in the night breeze. It was a glorious night to be alive.

After Everett departed Hopi land, he worked west to the Grand Canyon. In the four years he spent in this country, he visited the Grand Canyon three times, coming back again and again to partake of the rarified atmosphere of this place. At that time, the South Rim was known for its isolation and solitude. It was a place of clarity, and Everett wrote many letters there reflecting on the previous month's travel. To Ned, a friend, he wrote this letter, dated September 27, 1934:

> *In my wanderings this year I have taken more chances and had more wild adventures than ever before. And what magnificent country I have seen—wild, tremendous wasteland stretches, lost mesas, blue mountains rearing upward from the vermilion sand of the desert, canyons five feet wide at the bottom and hundreds of feet deep, cloudbursts roaring down unnamed canyons, and hundreds of houses of the cliff dwellers, abandoned a thousand years ago.*

Everett still possessed his enthusiastic and youthful point of view on his last visit here, yet his perspectives had been enlarged and enriched by the solitude and solace he found. Everett had arrived at a place within him where he was at peace with the world and himself.

Shortly before dawn, I was suddenly awakened by an airplane making a low run overhead. The plane's props were too loud, and I was frightened it might crash. I sat up quickly, half asleep and disoriented. The plane passed safely overhead, and I lay back down, curling potato-bug style.

The next thing I knew, I was lying on my back, hands clasped behind my head. I was listening to another low-flying plane parade by. I don't know how long I'd been lying there. Above me, the magnificent palette of blue sky greeted me fully awake. Across its length and width were the Monday-morning contrails. They crisscrossed and checkerboarded the sky like some big-time game of tic-tac-toe. I counted twelve unbroken jetliner contrails, stretching from horizon to horizon; another half dozen or so were in various stages of disintegration and floated unattached across the scene.

The Grand Canyon is directly below one of America's busiest flight paths. Every day people peer out porthole windows to catch a glimpse of the mighty Grand Canyon, some thirty-five thousand feet below. And every day, the Grand Canyon looks up to see and hear them go racing by.

Nearer to the ground, the local air traffic was getting worse. Every minute or so, another low-flying sightseeing plane lumbered by. Even when I couldn't see them, the drone of their engines carried me back to the places I sought to escape. It was time to get moving, so I climbed out of my sleeping bag and stood up.

I'm certain I wouldn't have slept as well as I did had I known I was lying in the middle of a garbage dump. Sitting at the base of a tree were four neatly folded plastic diapers. They were filled to the brim with natural goodness, just thirty feet away from a garbage can. Behind some low brush, I discovered wadded-up tissue paper and the toilet of the previous campers. Gruesome. Get your shovel, I said to myself. The ground was littered with paper, cigarette butts, plastic, and even a half-empty vial of insulin. From the cement fire pit I retrieved several large pieces of tinfoil, a dozen or so empty beer cans, some burnt plastic and tin containers, more cigarette butts, some candy wrappers, and a broken-down folding lawn chair.

"Thank god for national parks!" Mick said cynically, from the round table.

"Oh, yeah?" I said.

"Yeah. It keeps the people outta the wilderness."

"Yeah."

Later, at Grand Canyon Village I could not find a parking place. I needed supplies, but the parking lot was filled and the roadway on either side was lined with idling RVs. It reminded me of a railroad freight yard I worked at as a youth. I decided I would go without, but my escape route was blocked by an RV slowly inching up the highway. A bumper sticker plastered on its rear end offered this advice: "Burn Some Fossil Fuel Today; Put an American to Work."

EMERY KOLB'S BOATHOUSE

Over the years, the notion that Everett was never going to be found and would forever beckon me to return to this landscape had soothed and comforted me. But, all that took a dramatic about-face when in 1987 I happened on an old newspaper article about the unsolved disappearance of two adventurers and publicity seekers, Glen and Bessie Hyde, at the Grand Canyon in 1928.

It all started in the spring of 1928 when newlyweds Glen and Bessie Hyde decided to run the Colorado River from Green River, Utah, to Needles, California. They were a striking couple. Glen was ruggedly handsome and fancied himself an adventurer and explorer in the image of Admiral Byrd. The young Glen's confidence overshadowed his lack of experience and the peril the river would serve up. While Glen believed great adventures were in store for him, his lovely wife, Bessie, wanted to embrace the peace, beauty, and grandeur of the canyons. Bessie was an idealist and artist. Her language was poetry and her vocabulary consisted of paradox, metaphor, and analogy. With Glen's courageousness and Bessie's flare for writing, they would live the lives of adventurers, authors, and lecturers.

The way Glen figured it, their first big adventure would put their name on the map. Without wearing life jackets, they would navigate the Colorado River in a boat he built, thus assuring their fame and fortune. Besides, Bessie would then become the first woman to make the trip down the Colorado River.

On October 20, 1928, they set out from Green River, Utah, and twenty-eight days later they arrived at Bright Angel Trail at the South Rim of the Grand Canyon. They had negotiated some of the most treacherous rapids in the world, including the white water of Cataract Canyon in what is now Canyonlands National Park.

With Cataract behind them, Glen was cocksure they would have no trouble in the Grand Canyon. But by now, Bessie had great reservations about completing the trip. Her belief in her husband's invincibility had evaporated after Glen was knocked unconscious by an unmanned and out-of-control oar, then thrown overboard into the churning rapids of Cataract Canyon. Luckily, the current carried the boat near the unconscious Glen where Bessie was able to grasp him and hold on until the water calmed.

At the Grand Canyon's South Rim, the couple was met by journalists, photographers, and many well-known Grand Canyon river runners, including the famous photographer and river runner, Emery Kolb. After examining Hyde's boat, several seasoned boatmen, including Kolb, tried to convince the couple not to go farther. It was only dumb luck that they had survived so far, they said. The river was high, the boat was inadequate, and the idea of not wearing life jackets was pure craziness. Glen would have none of it. They had made it through Cataract Canyon, and nothing—especially the warnings from envious river runners—was going to stop him from completing the adventure.

Emery Kolb had arrived at the Grand Canyon at the turn of the century. He was the first person to carry a motion-picture camera down the canyon in 1912. His moving pictures and still photography are acknowledged as helping introduce the splendor of the canyon to the world. Known for his quick temper and foolhardy courage, Kolb spent his adult life photographing the canyon and operating a river-running company at the South Rim.

On the night before their departure down the canyon, Glen Hyde and Emery Kolb argued after Kolb suggested that Bessie be left behind. Witnesses later said the two men nearly came to blows before the argument ended. Early the next morning, Glen and Bessie pushed off to the cheers of a crowd that lined the shore. Later, one well-wisher reported that Bessie was very subdued, and another said that Glen had to force her onto the boat as they departed.

One month later, they had not arrived at the south end of the canyon. A search was mounted and led by Emery Kolb. After two weeks without a trace, Kolb and his party found the Hydes' boat peacefully floating in an alcove halfway down the canyon. Remarkably, the contents of the boat were dry and safely stowed away. It appeared that none of the food had been eaten. Whatever had happened to Glen and Bessie occurred shortly after their departure from the South Rim.

For years afterward, Kolb was suspected of being at the center of the couple's disappearance. It was rumored that Kolb and Bessie had been seen alone together shortly before the Hydes' departure. Though Kolb steadfastly denied any involvement in the couple's disappearance, over the years his argument with Glen was not dismissed.

Nearly a half century after the couple disappeared, Emery Kolb died in 1978. Authorities were shocked to discover the fully clothed remains of a man hidden in an old boat that was strapped to the ceiling of his boathouse. Law enforcement officials quickly concluded that the remains belonged to Glen Hyde and that they had solved part of the mystery of the Hydes' disappearance.

From the moment I heard about the remains in Kolb's boathouse, I had a gut-wrenching feeling that they did not belong to Glen Hyde at all but to Everett Ruess.

In the four-year period before Everett disappeared, he visited the South Rim of the Grand Canyon three times. Though Everett made no direct mention of Kolb in his letters, it would have been out of character for Everett not to have sought Kolb out and introduced himself. In a letter to his father, dated July 16, 1934, posted at the Grand Canyon, he wrote, "My life has continued as I have wished. I have made two more friends, with whom I had stimulating intellectual discourse, that broadened mental horizons. They were men of fine character both. A friend is indeed a wonderful treasure."

Could this have been a reference to Emery Kolb?

I learned from the Cocochino County, Arizona, authorities that only a handful of white men were known to have been in the Grand Canyon area during the 1920s, and of them, only Hyde had been reported missing. The authorities listened intently to my theory, but there was nothing they could do. They had no idea who the victim was, and Kolb was dead. Who would they prosecute? Regrettably, the victim's identity and the troubling circumstance surrounding the body's discovery would have to remain a mystery.

I then contacted nationally known forensic anthropologist Dr. Walter Birkby who had examined the remains. Birkby concluded that the remains were not those of Glen Hyde. Using computer technology, Birkby superimposed a head-shot photograph of Hyde over that of the skull found in Kolb's boathouse. Birkby concluded that the bone structure of the skull could not have been Glen Hyde's.

Birkby also told me what he knows about the person found in Kolb's boathouse. The person died from a single .32 caliber gunshot to the head. He was male, Caucasian, and between the ages of twenty and thirty. He stood approximately five feet seven inches tall and weighed approximately one hundred and forty pounds. He wore size nine shoes. From clothing and the condition of the body, Birkby estimated the person died between 1930 and 1935.

Everett Ruess was Caucasian. He was twenty years old when he disappeared. He stood five feet eight inches tall. He weighed one hundred and forty pounds. He wore size nine shoes. And he disappeared in 1934, just a few miles north of the Arizona-Utah border. One by one, the colorful pieces of a mosaic strewn over two states more than a half century earlier began to come together to form the outline of a tragic crime. Strangely, as these tiles began to fit into place, my need to disprove this new and impetuous theory grew and grew until it consumed me.

There is unsubstantiated evidence that Emery Kolb planned a photographic trip into the same approximate area where Everett disappeared at the same time. Whether or not Kolb made this trip is unknown. In the spring of 1935, after Everett's disappearance became known, Captain Neal Johnson found a paintbrush near Davis Gulch. Initially, this paintbrush was thought to have been Everett's, but after further investigation it was discovered that the paintbrush actually belonged to a white man who had been in the area making photographs in the late fall of 1934. Could this photographer have been Emery Kolb? There is little chance we will ever know since the man's identity was either never recorded or has been lost since.

Could it be that Emery Kolb was out on a photographic expedition and ran into Everett? After this meeting, could it be that Everett loaded his pack on the stronger and faster horses owned by Kolb and willingly went along with him, leaving his burros in Davis Gulch where he would return for them later? In all likelihood, Everett would not have turned down an opportunity to travel with the well-known and highly respected Kolb. Could it be that they traveled southwest together, crossing the Colorado River and traveling to the Grand Canyon before something happened?

All of the above is speculation, but two nagging questions remain: Whose body was found in Kolb's boathouse? If it wasn't Glen Hyde's and no other Anglo was reported missing during that period, just whose remains are they? Secondly, if Everett was killed or died naturally in the vicinity of Davis

Gulch, why didn't Dougi or any of the many searchers who have gone over that country since find his remains or his camp equipment?

What would Emery Kolb's motive be for killing Everett? It is well documented that Kolb had a serious mean streak and often used violence to solve problems. Perhaps after arriving at the Grand Canyon, Kolb and Everett had a disagreement, which resulted in Everett's death.

In another seemingly unrelated yet baffling occurrence during the winter of 1934–35, Kolb's brother, Ellsworth, mysteriously left the prosperous photographic and guide business that he and his brother operated at the Grand Canyon, and moved to California. Little is known about what prompted Ellsworth to leave, except that he and his brother had had a serious disagreement. Ellsworth refused to have anything further to do with Emery. Could it be that Ellsworth knew about the killing and refused to be a party to it?

It is also worth mentioning that, though Emery Kolb was married and had a daughter, he spent most of the time with men and often engaged in dangerous stunts to prove his manhood. There is no evidence that he was gay, yet the possibility is worthy of exploration. Could it be that Kolb was attracted to the young artistic Ruess? Further, after Kolb was rebuffed by Everett, could a violent struggle have ensued during which Everett was shot?

To take this line of reasoning one step further, could it be that one reason Everett was traveling alone in the desert was his attempt to understand his own sexuality? There are many references to girls and women in Everett's letters, so the likelihood of him being homosexual is remote. However, it should be noted that what we know about Everett today comes primarily from his letters and essays, and there is evidence that Everett did not always divulge everything about his life in his writings. For example, after a serious reaction to poison ivy in Zion National Park in 1932, Everett landed in the hospital, yet he failed to mention this to his family. Could it be that Everett had a secret life, a dual existence of sorts, a shadow side that was hidden from the rest of the world?

It would have been impossible for Everett to live and work as an artist in San Francisco without knowing many homosexuals. In a letter to his brother, Waldo, Everett wrote about his love of classical music, including this reference: "In Hollywood I knew of several people with fine orthophonic victrolas and whole cabinets full of symphonies, but all these people were either effeminately queer or impossible in some other way, so I did not hear their music."

Yet, in another letter, this one generated shortly after to a friend only identified as Fritz, he wrote, "I have several friends with fine victrolas and recorded music, and I have some myself and can borrow more."

Still, in another letter, this one to his dear friend Bill, Everett wrote, "I find that life is still awhirl, though no longer a swirl. I have, however, been on several Bacchic revels and musical orgies . . ."

In all likelihood, Everett's references were nothing more than a well-educated youth parading his knowledge of music and mythology, but again an examination of all possibilities is always worth the exploration. Hypothetically, if Kolb and Ruess were gay and met up out in the desert, a motive for Everett leaving his burros and his subsequent murder could be established.

CHAPTER TEN

EARTHFIRST!

Near the eastern boundary of Zion National Park, along the Paunsaugunt plateau side of the juniper- and cedar-topped White Cliffs, there is a dirt road where once a long time ago, I experienced the deepest and most soothing quiet I have ever known.

The only other time I've been on this road was with Mick. We had been new to the desert and found the road quite by accident one evening as we searched for campsites. While I spent only a few nights there, the importance of this place has continued to grow within me as the years have passed. When I'm far from home or experiencing one of life's excruciating miseries, an image of this place comes to me.

The image I have is not really an image at all; it is more a feeling that originates someplace within me. It might even be an obscure recollection of a long-lost state of being. I have a strong sense that I left something behind there, yet I'm certain I took something very important away with me. Not long ago, I returned to see just what it is that makes this place so special to me.

My return to this dirt road finds it in the last stages of decay. One day soon it will be gone; nature's reclamation will be complete. The wind, the water, and the passing of time will have erased the last remnants of man's intrusion.

Someone else had traveled this way recently; a set of tire tracks traced ahead of me into the road's curves and up its hills. The tracks led me into its obstacles and through its snake-like undulations. Flash floods had done a fairly good job of making driving difficult and dangerous. Rare storms had sent water channeling down the center of the road or cutting laterally through it. More than once I was forced to navigate a narrow path above deep V-shaped channels, one set of tires on either side. In other places I had to stop and remove debris from the roadway.

Within a few miles the going got even tougher. Four-wheel drive. Low range. I inched forward for nearly an hour before the road wound its way to the base of a 1,000-foot-high, three-tiered mesa. I got out of my vehicle and took a long look. It didn't look passable at all, but I proceeded anyway, starting up the first series of switchbacks where the road was cut into the talus slope and white sandstone cliff face. The deterioration was extreme; the road was narrow, rutted, and strewn with fist-sized rocks and boulders anchored to the ground. Erosion had weakened the roadbed in places, and it appeared it might collapse under the weight of my vehicle. In my imagination, I saw it crumbling away below me as I bounced up and over it. Unlike our day-to-day lives that allow us to stop and consider our next move, dangerous roads such as this do not afford that luxury. On these roads, once the decision is made to proceed, the driver is forced forward. He or she cannot go halfway or turn around. The driver must keep the engine's RPMs high or the motor will die. It is a scary-as-hell situation but not nearly as scary as the alternative.

Just as I crested the last ridge, I suddenly saw a man standing in the roadway in front of me! He was waving his arms back and forth frantically, trying to get my attention. "Outta the way, Imbecile!" I screamed, cranking my wheel left to avoid hitting him. This move sent me onto the crumbling shoulder and inches from plummeting off a 150-foot cliff. I snapped the wheel back to the right, and for an instant I had a sinking feeling that I may not have made it completely around the knucklehead in the roadway.

Cresting the ridge, I found a safe place to pull over. By the time I jumped out, the imbecile had arrived. Thank God, I didn't hit him. Before I could say a word, he thrust his hand out to me in friendship.

"Hey, dude, I'm Lance," he said, not waiting for me to offer my name. "Boy, am I glad to see you! We need help!" Lance was tall, lanky, and handsome. His long brown hair was tied in a ponytail and hidden under a red bandana that was folded into a triangle. He wore a black Grateful Dead T-shirt, baggy shorts, and Birkenstock-style sandals. Lance was not carrying water.

"Where's your water?" I asked, after introducing myself.

Lance didn't acknowledge my question. He was truly freaked out and pointed back up the road. "We got stuck, and I've gone for help. I've been walking hours." He leaned over at the waist, holding his stomach and attempting to control his breathing. "Will you help us, please?"

"Sure, if I can," I said. "But where is your water?"

"I don't have any. We drank it. That's part of the problem!"

Indeed. "Care for a sip?" I asked, holding out a bottle.

"Yeah, I could sure use it." Lance took the bottle and drank greedily.

A minute later, we were slowly making our way up the road to where his friends were waiting. Lance and his three companions—Michelle, Dan, and Shauna—were out from the East Coast. They had never seen anything like the desert and canyon country before, and they wanted to make this place their home. Lance was earnest, naive, and refreshing; he reminded me of the person Everett might have been, or perhaps even the person I might have been before JFK's assassination, the Vietnam War, and the traitor Nixon hastened the arrival of my cynicism.

"If there are four of you," I asked, "why are you out here alone?"

"I was the only one who could leave. Someone had to stay with the girls, so it was up to either Dan or me."

"Are Shauna and Michelle sick?"

"What?"

I rephrased my question. "Are the girls unable to walk? Why didn't one of them go along with you?"

"Oh yeah, they can walk . . . I don't know why . . . No one brought it up . . . I guess I was doing the manly thing," he said, smiling. "You know, taking care of the ladies."

"Is that what it means to be a man?"

Lance did not know how to answer my question. He was obviously uncomfortable and changed the subject.

"Do you know anything about EarthFirst!?"

I recognized something familiar in his voice; it had the same condescending nasal quality of the Scientologists. "Very little," I said, turning to face him, "but I suspect I'm going to learn more, right?"

Lance laughed nervously and asked how old I was. Without waiting for my answer, he launched into a campaign about the important work that EarthFirst! was doing. As he spoke, the zeal of the political apparatchik replaced the Scientologist's lament. Lance concluded with a proclamation, as is the case with most manifestos, "Yeah, I'm an EarthFirst! member. I just joined."

"Like I couldn't have guessed," I said in my best Jewish mother's voice.

Lance nodded up the road. "Someone has to do something. We can't just sit around and wait. The international mining companies and the cows are ruining it. We can't wait for someone else to do something!"

I knew the next comment I made would either end the testimonial or it would escalate it to another, more insidious level. "Yes, something needs to be done."

Lance smiled widely. "I just can't comprehend the morality of people who abuse this fantastic land."

Oh no! The morality word. I'd made a big, big mistake. Just when I hoped it was over, I had instead evoked the young preacher man in Lance.

For the next few minutes I was forced to endure the rhetoric of extreme: the land of black and white, the place where gradations, levels, nuances, and colorations do not exist. It didn't matter what side I listened to, it was all the same narrow fundamentalism. No perspective. No other side. No room for compromise.

Lance was practicing his land-use sermon on me. I had a strong urge to quickly reach past him, open the door, and push him out. I've always hated being a captive audience. Lance was watching my responses, gauging my reactions to his views. I yawned deeply, rubbed my eyes, looked at my wristwatch, and stared blankly out the window.

I would never let Lance know it, but I was in agreement with some of what he said. Middle-aged men do not want to listen to young men, even when they have something to say. I was no exception. I remembered being Lance's age and watching the frustration in older men's faces when I tried to dazzle them with brilliance or baffle them with bullshit. It was far easier talking to a young man than listening to one.

Nearing their camp, I spotted a VW bus in the trees; it was hopelessly mired up to its axles in the sand. Lance's friends were like him—young, good looking, and dressed in a similar fashion. Michelle and Shauna greeted Lance as though he were a real hero. They also greeted me warmly, but Dan remained aloof. He shook my hand, then moved back to X-ray me.

I pulled a large bottle of water from my vehicle, downed a couple of swallows, and noticed the group's Adam's apples bobbing up and down like gaggling turkey chicks. I handed the bottle to Michelle, and it quickly made the rounds. I retrieved another bottle, and it went around. It was difficult for me to fathom how these desert neophytes made it onto the plateau in a two-wheel-drive vehicle. Even more confusing was why they pulled out into the deep sand when white rimstone surrounded them.

"Anyone have a shovel?" I asked.

Silence.

"Okay, I do," I said. "Dan, how about straightening the front wheels, then digging behind both the front and rear wheels and axles." I handed Dan my trusty, fold-out, army-issue shovel. I gave Michelle and Shauna my aluminum bow saw and asked them to cut some cedar boughs. To Lance I said, "You and I will connect the tow chain from my front end to your rear end."

"All right!" Lance said, slapping me with a high-five.

After a few minutes of very intense, difficult, and frustrating work, their home on wheels sat safely atop an appendage of white rimstone. They were relieved, and the hopeful spirit that brought them to this place returned. This spirit excited me—it was a beautiful childlike thing; it was delicate and yet remarkably durable. More times than not, by the time a person reaches my age, this spirit is covered with a deep coating of tarnish or it has vanished altogether. Dan smiled widely at me, and his handsome face lit up, revealing his true boyish nature.

We stood marveling at the van for a long time before they climbed in and prepared to depart. Dan started the engine and turned the stereo on so loudly they were forced to shout to be heard. Lance leaned out the window and hollered, "It sure is quiet out here, Mark. It's really, really weird." He smiled at me.

Dan stuck his head out, too. "Hey, Mark, we're on our way to an environmental powwow; care to come along?"

"Thanks, Dan, but no. Fact is, I've got an appointment with Dr. Quiet up the road a few. Thanks, anyway."

After a quizzical look, Dan asked, "Doesn't the quiet get to you when you're out here alone?"

"Yes."

I quickly grabbed a gallon of water from my vehicle and handed it to Shauna through a window.

"Remember," I yelled, over the music, "never, ever go into the desert without water! Lots and lots of water. In case of emergency."

Two hours later, I stood at the center of my long-ago campsite. I had made good on my promise to return one day. Very little looked familiar, but as I moved around, standing in one place and then another, it all started coming back to me. To the northwest, Zion's white and pink cathedrals rose up like giants of truth, towering above the clean green forest surrounding them. To the northeast and east, a mesa near the Kaiparowits Plateau arced away into obscurity, its cliff line unbroken and stretching nearly fifty miles before disappearing into the bowels of the earth. Nearest me, the cliffs seemed to radiate or glow with an inner light. Behind me to the south, the mysterious cedar-covered hills called out to me, beckoning.

It was very hot, at least 100 degrees. It was hot when Mick and I were there, too. The mixture of extreme heat and deep quiet is a very volatile concoction, and it quickly collapsed all my defenses and forced me to acknowledge the numbing emptiness within me. This is a very dangerous place; truth can be uttered in this heady environment, and it will be heard on a cellular level. I stood down in place. I sensed something happening within me. It was the roiling sea of tears. The tide was rising up to meet the quiet and heat of the place. I would make my stand here and let the sea of tears have its way with me—for I could do little to stop it even if I cared to.

I had never felt so utterly alone as I did then.

After a long time, I let my legs carry me south into the cedar forest and towards a circle of freestanding boulders I could see about a half-hour's walk away. From my vantage point the giant boulders formed a Stonehenge-like enclosure but on a much grander natural scale. When I finally reached the circle of stones and passed between its perfectly matched boulders, a strange realization swept over me.

I'd been here before! I knew this place! Mick and I were here!

I moved quickly forward letting my legs and body carry me around trees, bushes, rocks, and obstacles. My body seemed to know where it was going, but my intellect was a click or two behind; I was only able to acknowledge things a moment or two after they happened. My arms swept back and forth as I walked. They reminded me of the arms of some great timepiece from another world. Somehow, I was a participant and a spectator in this experience. Waves of euphoria rushed in on me from all directions. I felt good now, very good indeed! I sensed I was moving forward into a dissolution of my individual self toward a union with the serenity of the natural world.

Suddenly, before I knew what was happening, I had stopped and was standing over The Horse With No Name. I couldn't believe it! How could I forget? How in the world could I ever forget The Horse With No Name?

The horse was laying in the sand just as Mick and I had left him so long ago. His sun-bleached bones were now half buried in the vermilion-colored sand. It was a striking image: white-on-white bone mingling with mercuric red sand. I felt weak and sick to my stomach.

How could I *ever* forget?

Years ago when Mick and I stood here, the palomino had been dead for only a short time. Its leathery hide was semi-supple, its long white mane was thick and beautiful, and its handsome face showed great nobility. Mick and I named our companion The Horse With No Name after the song by the group America that was popular at the time.

Strangely, the horse was still as striking and beautiful as it was so long ago. Its power and elegance, its spirit and sweet nature had somehow survived death. This seemed particularly odd to me since I had changed so much over the intervening years. I had crossed so many thresholds and experienced so many incarnations that I no longer remembered who I really was back then.

I did remember that on the evening Mick and I spent there, the sunset seemed to dissolve the world around us in an unearthly pink glow. Mick and I were in a solemn mood at first, and we toasted the horse with vodka straight from the bottle. It was sad that this magnificent animal ever had to die out there alone. We went round and round and round the horse, postulating theories about how it might have gotten there and what might have happened to it. We ended up laughing wildly, slapping each other on the back, falling repeatedly to the ground, and singing lustily to our new friend.

I decided to break the smooth surface of the silence again. I would sing to the horse once more.

> *"Oh, I've been through the desert*
> *On a horse with no name.*
> *It felt good to be out of the rain.*
> *In the desert, you can't remember your name*
> *'Cause there ain't no one for to give you no pain . . ."*

As the words left my mouth, I was stricken by the sheer power and immensity of the silence. When it comes to transcendence, silence is more powerful than the rivers or the oceans or the mountains or the deep winding canyons. Silence can be terrifying, and this particular one was waiting for me to do something. I didn't know which way to turn.

I remembered that as Mick and I circled the horse, we dug a deep pathway around it in the sand. I looked to find the pathway now, but it was gone. The wind of eternity had covered it with the sands of time. Mick and I were so young back then. We were as unfamiliar with the mysteries of life as we were with the mysteries of death. I wished Mick could have been with me again on this fine evening so many years later. I wanted so badly to share the love and brotherhood once again that passed between us so long ago.

I circled The Horse With No Name as Mick and I once did. I listened for Mick's voice, speaking to me from the round table.

Silence.

"Certainly," I said aloud, frightening myself with the sound of my own voice, "on such an auspicious occasion, you will join the horse and me, won't you?"

Silence.

I turned in a tight circle and corkscrewed myself deep into the sand.

"Surely, my friend, you could join us, the horse and I, if only to put me down."

Silence.

Sunset.

Then it occurred to me. Though I could not hear Mick, I could feel him. For the very first time, I began to feel at peace about the immortality of my loved ones at the round table. We were together on this landscape forever.

Nothing could separate us here. Everything was as I have always wanted it to be. There was no reason to be fearful, no reason for me to grieve so. The sound of silence is the deepest vibration from eternity. It reaches from the center of my being to the furthermost star with the greatest of ease. It is the only substance that connects me and my world to the cosmic order of the universe.

Taking my shoes and socks off I slowly walked around the horse. The sand was still warm from the hot day, and it felt good against my skin. The sand oozed between my toes and up around my ankles. I looked down and my feet and ankles were gone, submerged in the deep luxuriant earth.

A line from one of Everett's letters came to me: *What a magnificent time to LIVE!*

It was Tasupi time and the sun had set below the horizon, yet the colors were still brilliant as they mixed and moved about Zion's cathedrals, filling the forest with magic. I circled the horse again and again, enjoying my homecoming long after darkness. I was unprepared to stay the night, but I was unwilling to leave. It had taken years to get back to this place, and I would not depart until I was ready. I made a fire and continued my celebration.

I danced and sang long into the night, and when weariness finally overtook me, I lay down on my back in the sand. To my left The Horse With No Name was watching me, and to my right the fire burned down into white and gold embers. Above me, the silent stars watched over me like great mothers of the sky.

I was not alone.

In the morning, I packed and left. Before I did, I returned to the circle of stones and The Horse With No Name. It was time for another good-bye. I didn't suppose I'd ever be back this way again.

There are places or junctures in each person's life where he or she must strike out anew, forever leaving previous lives behind. The Horse with No Name was one of the places for me. Like some alchemist's secret process, this land of silence turned my pain and confusion into hope and serenity.

When Mick and I had first arrived there, I was a very troubled and melancholy boy; my life was in shambles. When I departed a few days later, I possessed a sense of equanimity and peace that still lives within me today. Over the years I have grown into manhood, and somewhere along the way I discovered that when my sense of peace grows dim, I can return here and replenish it. I learned as Everett did that the healing power of nature not only soothes and comforts, but it rekindles the fire of life.

Since that one evening so very long ago, I have really never left my beloved desert silence for very long. I have made hundreds of pilgrimages to my land of transcendence. Solace and truth await me here. It is my cathedral and church, my philosopher's stone, and my treasure at the end of the rainbow.

I will not drive that dirt road again. That road needs to vanish. I have used the dirt roads of this country my entire life, and I see their curves and holes and dry washes in my dreams. I have relied on these roads to carry me forward in life and to carry me back to places and feelings I love.

At about the same time Everett wandered here, the land was being cut up and bisected by these roads. Using bulldozers, prospectors explored this outback, plowing across it in every direction, stacking their manhood into piles like the centuries-old cedars they uprooted and discarded in their wake. The soft sandstone was no match for these explorers; a million years of erosion could now be accomplished in one afternoon. Most of these roads were used just once. Miners pushed these roads into the most isolated spots they could find to drill a single exploratory shaft. If it weren't for the highest mesas, the deepest canyons, and some of the most difficult terrain on earth, nothing could have stopped them.

There were success stories such as that of Charlie Steen, the penniless prospector who became a millionaire during the first generation of American atomic paranoiacs. He and a few others found rich deposits of uranium, and his jackpot set off a land rush during which most of canyon country was ruthlessly explored and posted. The archaeological relics of this period that I call the Prospector Age are everywhere. Some mining camps remain today exactly as they did when their builders walked away.

Steen's good luck nurtured a hope of new prosperity within the communities surrounding this unique land. But as time passed, this prosperity did not materialize, and local economies stagnated, falling into decay. Many people were forced to leave, yet many others stayed behind, hoping the desert outback might be their salvation. Despite the rarity of the rags-to-riches stories such as that of Charlie Steen and the heightened awareness about environmental matters, the people of this area are still waiting and hoping today.

The Prospector Age is coming to a close, but its legacy—the more than 5,000 dirt roads left behind—remains. These roads are at the center of the current land war. It all boils down to this: he who controls the roads or access to the land controls the future of the land. The great blocks of undisturbed land are gone; only pieces remain. Each of these pieces owes its shape and size to the dirt roads surrounding it, and each piece is being fiercely fought over by people who believe they have a manifest right to it.

I, for one, must change my ways. It is not easy to change, but it is necessary. Once, I collected Anasazi artifacts, mostly pieces of flint or bits of pottery and, if I was really lucky, an arrowhead. I have stopped taking these objects when I find them. I have returned the treasures I collected to the land. Recently, I found a secret Anasazi ruin on Cedar Mesa. It contained two bowls, a tall artistically painted pot, and a half dozen sandals woven from reeds. I must have been the first white man ever to find this ruin, I reasoned; why else would the artifacts still be there? The truth is, I really wanted to take these treasures. I finally left the ruin as I had found it.

Another thing—one day soon I will reluctantly build my last fire ring. On that day, I will collect only perfect stones and assemble them into a perfect circle. I will build a fire of cedar and juniper, and I will breathe in its sweet fragrance. I will watch the flames curl into the night sky, carrying me away.

EVERETT'S DISAPPEARANCE

Over the years several people allegedly bragged about killing Everett Ruess. Of these confessions, mostly alcohol-induced, two are particularly noteworthy.

The first alleged confession came from an Anglo cowboy who lived in Escalante and who was a suspected cattle rustler working on the range near Davis Gulch when Everett disappeared. He was considered by many to be mean enough to kill and is reported to have told people, "I killed the goddamned artist kid and threw his body in the Colorado River." Some in Escalante are convinced he was the murderer.

The second man who reportedly confessed to killing Everett was Jack Crank. He was a secretive man who spent most of his life hiding out in the wilderness, so today little is known or remains to be discovered about him. What is known is that by the time Crank was in his twenties, his fellow Native Americans would have nothing to do with him. Crank claimed he was Navajo, but Navajos insist he was Apache. The Apache say, No way, Crank was Navajo! One Hopi elder in Flagstaff, Arizona, told me, "When I was a boy, Crank was the most feared man known to my people. 'Never turn your back on Jack Crank,' people would say." The elder had seen Crank only a few times many years ago as a child, but he remembered the hate in Crank's eyes. "Jack Crank hated everyone, especially white men."

Crank drew himself into the mystery of Everett's disappearance in 1941 when he was jailed for the murder of a white man in Monument Valley. While in jail, Crank implicated two accomplices in the crime who, in turn, denied all involvement but told officials that years earlier Crank had admitted killing a "lone white man" in the country above Rainbow Bridge. The two men said that Crank killed the man because he needed the scalp of a "blood enemy" and because he hated whites. After killing the man, Crank was alleged to have taken his scalp and valuables and then buried him. He left the camp untouched but took the man's burros some distance away and placed them in a corral.

According to documents written by Indian Services Superintendent E. R. Fryer in 1942, Jack Crank bragged in detail of murdering Everett Ruess. Fryer wrote that evidence at hand and many peculiarities relative to the case made it appear that he was indeed the killer. Crank was never charged with the death of Everett and was released from prison in 1951. After his release for the murder in Monument Valley, no one remembers seeing Crank again.

When Jack Crank is considered a serious suspect in Everett's disappearance, some of the confusing and even mysterious elements relating to his disappearance and subsequent searches make more sense.

Remember what the Navajo medicine man, Natani, and his psychic wife told journalist John Terrell and Captain Neal Johnson during their late-night counsel? Terrell wrote:

> *In the sand she built a mound; she indicated crooked lines running from it. I knew then that she was building Navajo Mountain. . . . They [the lines] were the Colorado and San Juan Rivers." . . . Natani said, "Go to the forks of the rivers. . . . He was there. Close by he made a camp. You will find the fire . . ."*

Go to the forks of the rivers, Natani told them. In 1935, this was interpreted to mean Davis Gulch; that's where Everett's burros were located and where his campsites and footprints were found. While Davis Gulch is in the same general area as the confluence of the two great rivers, it is actually more than eight miles away to the north. On the other hand, Jack Crank's assertion that he killed a lone white man above Rainbow Bridge places the scene of his murder exactly at the confluence of the two rivers. Rainbow Bridge is one mile below the confluence of the Colorado and San Juan Rivers. Crank's alleged murder occurred at the exact place Natani and his wife said to go search.

What Natani said next to Terrell is prophetic:

> *"He [Everett] went away and does not mean to come back."*

> *"He went away without his camp outfit?" Terrell asked.*

> *"I do not see that clearly," Natani said. "There is a shadow. Only some of his outfit was moved away. There is more some place."*

At the time, Natani's prediction that some of Everett's camp equipment remained behind "some place" never panned out. I believe nothing was found because the searches were inadequate. I am also convinced that the famed tracker Dougi knew more than he said and that he intentionally led Terrell and Johnson away from the real scene.

In the concluding paragraph of John Upton Terrell's four-part series into Everett's mysterious disappearance, he wrote:

This is the result [of his investigation]: Everett Ruess was murdered in the vicinity of Davis Canyon. His valuable outfit was stolen. He never reached the Colorado River. But some day pieces of his outfit will turn up. Then, we shall take up the trail again.

Remarkably, in 1957, twenty-two years after Everett's disappearance, a fully equipped camp was discovered by two geologists working on the Glen Canyon Dam project in Reflection Canyon. This discovery could be the single most intriguing piece of evidence proving that Everett made it out of Davis Gulch; that he did not travel the route that Dougi and the searchers suspected into Navajo land; and finally, that Jack Crank was indeed linked to his disappearance.

Most importantly, Reflection Canyon is located at Natani's ground zero: it overlooks the confluence of the Colorado and San Juan Rivers. Standing on the ridge above the canyon, I can almost see Rainbow Bridge a mile to the south.

The camp equipment found in Reflection Canyon included a cup, plate, pots, pans, and a large canteen. They were all rusted out, filled with sand, and had obviously been there for many years. When the two geologists stumbled into the camp, they said it appeared as though someone had walked off and simply never come back. The frying pan was sitting at the edge of a fire ring and a metal cup and spoon sat on a rock nearby. Why would anyone discard important and expensive camp equipment, especially a canteen, so far out in the inhospitable desert? At the time, this equipment was essential for survival.

Some people are convinced that this camp outfit is Everett's, especially because of one item found there. Sitting at the base of a rock, protected from the weather, was a box of razor blades. The box of razor blades was a product of the Owl Drug Company of Los Angeles, located near the Ruess family home. It was also of a 1930s vintage. When Utah authorities shipped some of the camp equipment to Los Angeles for Stella and Christopher Ruess to inspect, the Ruesses could not be certain. They were now very old and many years had passed since their son's disappearance. Ultimately, the Ruess family concluded the items were not Everett's and no record of any further investigation existed.

Could it be that after Everett camped in Davis Gulch, he went south to Reflection Canyon where he met his demise at the hands of Jack Crank? Reflection Canyon lies in a direct line south from Davis Gulch heading toward Rainbow Bridge. This route follows an old Anasazi trail that was used by the Navajo, but because of its difficulty, it was abandoned in favor of the easier route onto Navajo land to the east. This easier route was the only one considered by searchers, including Dougi, who found no trace of Everett along its length.

It is possible that Everett went from Davis Gulch to Reflection Canyon where he planned to ford the Colorado River somewhere near Rainbow Bridge. There is, in fact, a famous river crossing just below Rainbow Bridge called San Benito Sausipuedes. It is the only place for many miles where the Colorado River widens to the point of becoming shallow enough for men and animals to cross. In November 1776, the Dominguez-Escalante Expedition learned of the crossing from some Indians after a week of unsuccessfully attempting to cross the river. The name San Benito Sausipuedes gives an indication of how members felt at the time. *San Benito* is the colorful red cassock worn by priests who were marked for punishment. The word *Sausipuedes* means "Get out if you can." From Rainbow Bridge, Everett would work back over the Bernheimer Trail around the western side of Navajo Mountain and ultimately end up at the Grand Canyon.

Jack Crank allegedly told people that after the killing, he left the camp but took the man's burros. Later, he left the burros in another canyon, fearing they would connect him to the murder. Could it be that Jack Crank traveled north after killing Everett and unwittingly—or cunningly—returned the burros back to Davis Gulch where Everett had made his earlier camp? If this were true, the confusion surrounding his burros being found there but not his camp equipment would make sense.

If Crank's story is true, Everett is buried somewhere in Reflection Canyon. When I return that way, I will trace back along what could have been Everett's last path into the canyon and see what I can dig up.

From the Grand Canyon, Everett worked north into Utah and the heart of sandstone canyon country to Bryce Canyon National Park. It was a long and difficult trek, but the beauty and solace of the changing seasons enraptured Everett. Autumn descended early onto the high country in 1934, and as Everett made his way from Bryce Canyon's lofty heights to the valleys of the Escalante Drainage, snow and colder weather accompanied him. The adventures of summer were over, and Everett looked forward to new adventures, wintering in the deep canyons of the Escalante.

ESCALANTE, UTAH

I arrived in town just after dusk, at the moment when shadows and secrets reveal themselves. I had just received word that my friend Nancy was dying. Stricken by this news, I planned to spend the night in Escalante then travel to Salt Lake City early the next morning to be with her. The eerie silence of Escalante added to my depression over losing another friend. No one was on the street, and I couldn't see a single electric light burning anywhere. I checked into a sleepy motel and found myself standing impatiently in my room's open doorway, staring out onto Main Street. The town appeared deserted, and I was restless. I pulled on my hiking boots and walked to Gail Bailey's old house.

Bailey is long gone, and the secret—if there ever was one—about what he found in Davis Gulch has gone on with him. I stood in front of his house for a long time until a neighbor's dog started barking. I continued on to George Davis's house and then finally to Jennings Allen's. The full moon rested above the eastern horizon and illuminated the houses on one side, casting eerie black shadows on the other.

I walked to the cemetery, and with the help of my trusty flashlight, I found most of the searcher's headstones. They are lying there in rows, together in death as they were in life.

Not long ago, an Escalante man told me he could prove Everett's personal belongings ended up in Escalante. He could supply me with evidence to prove his claim. Though he had not seen the evidence himself, a trusted old-timer he knew was in possession of some of Everett's drawings and letters. This old-timer told him that Everett was killed by a local man. The killer's identity was well known in Escalante. According to him, apparently, after the three quasi-official searches were concluded and the heat died down, it became common knowledge in the hamlet who the murderer really was.

When I spoke with the old-timer, he was suspicious. He had agreed to meet me specifically to talk about Everett, but then he denied knowing anything about him at all. Finally, I called his bluff, "You don't know a damn thing," I said, impatiently, "you're all blow and no go."

"By god, I know what I say is true!" he said, bristling with anger. "I've seen the goddamned pictures and the letters myself! I know what I'm talking about!"

The man admitted he had proof. He would show it to me. We agreed to meet later, but when I arrived at our meeting place, he never showed.

While there exists the real possibility that this unnamed Escalante cowboy or the renegade Navajo Jack Crank or even the famed photographer Emery Kolb killed Everett Ruess, there is still a much greater probability that Everett went out exploring one fine morning and did not return to his camp that night. Everett most likely died as he lived, seeking out the unknown places—both within and without—and living life to the fullest. I believe that the campsite found in Reflection Canyon in 1957 is Everett's last camp. I am also convinced that the Navajo tracker Dougi knew much more than he told officials or John Terrell. Dougi knew there was another trail Everett could have taken south out of Davis Gulch, but he never told anyone else. The question remains, why?

From the cemetery, I walked aimlessly around town until I ended up back on Main Street standing in front of the town's old movie house. On his last night in town, Everett and a few locals came to the theater and watched a Hollywood film, *Death Takes a Holiday*. Everett must have stood right here, I thought, where I am standing. The theater closed its doors decades ago, and in the moonlight it wore the forlorn face of all things once treasured but now forsaken. I circled around the building, admiring its original integrity and woodwork.

The back door was unlocked.

I pulled the door open and with the help of my flashlight, I worked past piles of boxes and junk stored in the building's rear and out into the theater's seating area. The room was big and hollow; the sound of my every move was amplified and reverberated. The dreams and images that lingered there must be in a deep slumber. I sat on the floor against a wall and turned my light off. I would wait and see what might happen. After a long time, I thought I sensed Everett's presence, yet I was not sure.

"Trust me," Mick said loudly from somewhere on the other side of the black room, "you will not find what you are looking for here."

Without discussion or hesitation, I turned my light back on, got to my feet, and quickly left. I pulled the door tightly closed behind me.

Standing back on the sidewalk, the moonlight cast my shadow onto the cement before me. A thought occurred to me. I have grown into manhood essentially alone. It has been a long journey, more than twenty-five years. My descent ended long ago, but my ascent has been long and arduous. I have come a long way, and I have even farther to go. I have lived twice as long as Everett, and I know much more than he did about growing into manhood.

I have often worried about the Hopi and Dineh boys I have met, and the difficult path to manhood that lies before them. I am also very worried about the journey that Anglo boys from my culture—especially my sons—are making into manhood. While the Dineh and Hopi have traditions, rituals, and the understanding of family and tribe, my Anglo culture possesses none of this. We have washed our hands of the work that makes boys into men. Sadly, the connection between boys and healthy, mature men has been all but severed. One day soon, perhaps, no men will live in America.

It was *Nuptu*, the Hopi word for the pre-dawn "purple light of creation," and I wandered all the way to the Escalante River in the ancient grove of cottonwood trees where Everett camped. I had returned to the place my search began. A full circle. I know much more than when I began, especially about my own undefined quest or journey. I had not solved the mystery of Everett's disappearance, and in the new morning light, this gave me considerable satisfaction despite my nagging pain over Nancy. Some mysteries belong unsolved—beckoning us forward, haunting us until we strike out on our own.

Everett transcended the whirl of modern life and experienced periods of enlightenment. He ventured further into the realm of nature's magic than most of us will ever know. While Everett was only partially aware of what was happening to him, he had an overwhelming desire to share it with others. He believed that if he could just communicate it to others, they, too, might be able to share in its magic and wonder. In May 1934, Everett wrote this letter, the addressee is unknown. I like to think he wrote it for me.

> *I have been fighting my way up tall hills, between canyons of skyscrapers, hurling myself against the battling night winds, the raw, swooping gusts that are like cold steel on my cheeks. I am drunk with a searing intoxication that liquor could never bring—drunk with the fiery elixir of beauty, the destroying draught of power, and the soul piercing inevitability of music.*

> *Often I am tortured to think that what I so deeply feel must always remain, for the most part, unshared, uncommunicated. Yet, at least I have felt, have heard and seen and known, beauty that is inconceivable, that no words and no creative mediums are able to convey. Knowing that the cards are stacked, and realizing achievements are mere shadows of the dream, I still try to give some faint but tangible suggestion of what has burned without destroying me.*

> *But I realize that what I have felt must grow within one, and it is folly that will be scorned and misinterpreted to seek to tell of it.*

> *Such is my cry, such is my plaint, and I know there is no reply. Mine seems a task essentially futile. Try as I may, I have never yet, that I know of, succeeded in conveying more than a glimpse of my visions. . . . I am torn by the knowledge that what I have felt cannot be given to another.*

Rest easy, my friend. You have given much beauty, joy, and enlightenment to many. The seasons will come and the seasons will go, and your visions will be celebrated again and again.

CHAPTER TWELVE

SALT LAKE CITY

I didn't arrive in Salt Lake City until after dark, but I went directly to Nancy's parents' house where she was being cared for and receiving her last visitors. As I made my way along the roads I've driven for years, I began to feel uncomfortable. My discomfort stemmed from Nancy's dire circumstances, but there was something else, too. Nothing around me looked familiar. Bit by bit, piece by piece, my hometown had been torn down. Almost every structure of historic or architectural significance was gone. Standing where these valued members of the community once stood were new, temporary-looking strip malls and fast-food eateries. If the message of architecture built during Everett's day spoke of permanence and strength, its message today surely speaks of impermanence and facade.

Long before I arrived with my provisional claims of ownership, the neighborhood where I was raised had been farmland for nearly one hundred years. When my young parents and their generation arrived here, it was to start a new life after the Great Depression and World War II. They possessed a utopian dream that could be summed up in one word: suburbs. Only the centers of the aging neighborhoods they built remain today; the rest are in the development loop. Until recently, rural and urban lifestyles coexisted in Salt Lake Valley, but those days are gone.

On my way to Nancy's parents, I veered into the old neighborhood and drove by Sylvia Knight's house. Since Sylvia's death, I have driven by her place a thousand times. Once, long ago on a warm summer evening, Sylvia sneaked out of the house and met me around the corner a few houses away. It happened right there, I said to myself. She climbed on the back of my motorcycle, wrapped her arms around my middle, and we raced up Big Cottonwood Canyon. About halfway up the canyon, we stopped at The Stairs picnic area where we sat on a wooden table and talked. We were so young and naive. We were intoxicated by the moonlight and barely able to grasp reality out of the deep magic and wonder that comprised our young lives.

Next, I swung by Randall Pott's house, but along the way I was shocked to see that the historic Mormon church on Vine Street had been leveled. Even worse, the 100-year-old pine trees surrounding the church were gone. The autumn winds would no longer sing from the tops of the stately pines, inviting admirers to muse, and no spring birds would build nests there ever again. These trees had shaded generations of thankful worshipers and had given comfort to the sorrows of many. They had now received their thanks. While the church and especially its trees were gone forever, they exist yet, layered in the archaeology of my personal memory. I would not forget.

For an instant, as I rounded the corner to Randall Pott's old house, I thought I saw him sitting there on the steps, waiting for me. The house was still there, the steps were still there, the exact place Randall sat was there too, but he was gone. I'd been thinking, Just because you don't believe in a God, or you have rejected organized religion, or you are just feeling upside down about the whole thing and don't know what to think, it doesn't necessarily mean you can't believe in life after death.

As long as my memory is intact and working, the people I have shared my life with will live on within me. In a way, I carry the standard for all of us now. As long as I live, we all live. To make this work, for me at least, I must think of my dead friends often. I have a responsibility to remember their faces and their ideas; by speaking their ideas aloud and sharing them with others, they live on in a life after death. If I honor them by doing this, I honor myself and we all remain alive.

Far too much emphasis is placed on getting on with one's life after a loved one has died. Yes, we must continue on with our lives, but we are mistaken if we believe a loved one's life and death does not impact or influence our present and future. Furthermore, by denying our pasts, we close off access to the lessons and experiences that contribute to whom we are now. The threads of our soul are woven of a continuity between past, present, and future. It cannot be unraveled because joy has now turned to sorrow. Like the Cheyenne Indians who believe they must speak the names of their dead loved ones aloud, I must do the same. I will let their names roll off my lips and make the silence echo with their caress. If I do this, my sorrow has its reward.

A few blocks farther south I weaved by Mick's old house. He was not there anymore, yet some of his energy lingered. My route also took me by my parents' place, the house where I grew up.

At Nancy's childhood home, her family ushered me into her old bedroom. Nancy did not move as I entered; her frail, ghostly thin silhouette was barely visible under the blankets of the sterile-looking hospital bed. The sight of her lying there contradicted an image I had of her and her room from many years ago. For an instant, I could see Nancy and her best friend, Sylvia Knight, bouncing up and down on the bed. They were looking at me and giggling as high school girls do. They were so young and beautiful, so filled with life. Who could have known then what the future had in store for them?

Nancy's room was much smaller and darker than I remembered it. The drapes were closed, and the only light came from the hallway. Nancy had been given a drug prescribed for cancer patients in the last few hours of life. It was a tranquilizer that reportedly makes the individual feel at peace. Nancy neither moved when I sat on the edge of her bed nor when I took her hands in mine. I called out her name softly, and she began to writhe: her arms and legs flailed pathetically, her head turned from side to side, her lips mouthed words but did not have the wind for sound. Nancy was trying to say something to me but could not make it back from the drug-induced netherworld.

From the kitchen, Nancy's sister and husband spoke of her in the past tense. They discussed funeral arrangements. I leaned forward, brushed her hair away from her face, and studied her. I pressed her image between two blank pages in the archaeological file of my memory, the way one presses a beautiful, delicate rose.

"Hey, Nanc," I said in my clearest, most manly voice, "do you remember what we were doing a year ago today?"

She did not acknowledge.

"We were having dinner and drinks at the Dodo Restaurant. I'll never forget how much we laughed that night." I sat upright, laughing in the way of old friends, but inside I felt vacuous. The breath that precedes tears rose up in my chest like an inflatable balloon.

"Oh God, Nancy, I don't know what I'll do without you. I love you."

Again, Nancy tried to fight to the surface but could not make it. I sat quietly for a long time, studying every facet of her hands. I looked to see if anyone was watching, and when I saw they were not, I kissed her on the lips as I did for the first time twenty-five years ago. I kissed her the way a man kisses a woman he loves. I kissed her in desperation, knowing I would never kiss her again. I took a deep breath and committed her sweet fragrance to memory. Though ravaged by cancer and in the throes of death, Nancy remained one of the most beautiful and striking women I have ever known.

Nancy's mother was standing in the doorway; her silhouette darkened the already darkened room.

"Well, Nancy," I finally said, taking her hands in mine, "I wish I could just pick you up, carry you outside, and drive you down to the desert where we could turn our faces into the sunshine."

Suddenly, Nancy opened her eyes and looked directly into mine. In a clear, soft voice she slowly said, "Yes, Mark! I really like that idea." Just as quickly as it happened, it was over. Nancy closed her eyes and fell back into semiconsciousness.

A few minutes later I left, driving back across a town I had spent most of my life in but no longer knew or much cared about.

The next morning, Nancy died at the exact moment the sun broke over Mount Olympus. She was thirty-eight years young.

ABOVE DAVIS GULCH

I stood on a rock above Everett's last-known campsite. It was sunset on a breathtaking November evening almost sixty years to the day since he disappeared near there. Below me in the gulch all my friends were gathered around a campfire I had built in Everett's last-known fire ring. My friends were calling out to me, "Come down and join us!"

"I'll be down in a minute," I said.

On the southern horizon, Navajo Mountain turned slightly to address the coming night. The mountain's feet were submerged in blackness, and its broad shoulders were cloaked in shadow, yet its face burned with great nobility. To the west, I traced a line over the serrated horizon of Fifty Mile Ridge high above. The goldish-blue sunset backlit the ridge's cliff line, making every tree, rock, and pinnacle stand out in contrasting detail.

Tomorrow, I would get up before dawn, prepare as best I could, and hike to the top of the escarpment. There was no trail to the top of the ridge. Few have ever made the ascent; each person must pick his or her own way there. I had no idea what awaited me on top, but my expectations were high.

Turning to leave, something caught my eye. Out on the line between heaven and earth, the silhouette of a face began to form. One by one, each facial feature appeared like magic; they were perfect to the minutest detail. It was my friend Everett Ruess! I had been waiting and watching for this moment for a long time. Everett was smiling, and his lips seemed to reach up, tenderly kissing the heavens above. The wind swirled around my head, and I felt almost giddy.

So, Everett Ruess did make it back home after all! He is now part of the land he loved so intensely. All I could do was stand silently and smile. I was truly humbled. . . . Within a short time, the sunset faded, and Everett's silhouette returned to hiding. Just as I was about to leave, I thought I heard his voice calling out to me, but when I faced the direction of the sound, it was only the wind.

"Good night, Everett."

Turning away from the ridge, I walked down through the deep charcoal dusk into the light of the campfire and into the arms of the people who loved me. We would join hands and circle the campfire tonight. We would go round and round and round, digging a deep pathway into the soft sand. We would laugh and cry and reminisce. "How quickly the campfire burns low," someone would say. "How swiftly the years go racing by."

That night we would drink to love and friendship. We would toast our lives and our many passions.

Secretly, I would watch as our shadows danced and played on the surrounding canyon walls. When no one was looking, I would pull two clean sheets of white paper from the book of my archaeology and imprint *all* the light and *all* the shadow I found there.

What a magnificent time to live!

Mark A. Taylor is a novelist, investigative journalist, editor, essayist, and lecturer. He lives and works in the West, writing about the land and its people. Taylor had published in *Esquire* and *Penthouse* and has also published the novel *Chaco: A Tale of Ancient Lives*. He is the founder and publisher of the critically acclaimed art and literary journal *Ne-ol-o-gism*.